The
Dream Weaver
Chronicles

The Dream Weaver Chronicles

James Paul Davis

ECKANKAR
Minneapolis, MN

Contents

Acknowledgments

Deep thanks to these nine Brothers of the Leaf who had the pluck to join me on the vision quest: Alex, Anne, Ed, Jack, Jim, Kate, Kristin, Lila, and Maureen.

And a word of appreciation to my cat Gili, who sat on my lap and kept me company in the midnight hours while I wrote this book.

Introduction

Great moments in history transcend the skein of time, soaring high over the unfolding human drama to inspire future generations. When such moments occur at the threshold of a new age, they are twice endowed and become the stuff of legends. The building of the Temple of ECK was such a moment.

Lesser events burst forth upon the stage of life and, with much bravado, grab the headlines of the day. But they as quickly fade away, to be forgotten by all but the most studious historians. Meanwhile, behind the noise at center stage, the story of future legends quietly unfolds.

The construction of the Temple of ECK began in 1989. It was a year to be savored by ECKists. Yet to the world at large, the building of the Temple would appear as a minor footnote in a year that saw extraordinary changes sweep the world. I believe that few outside of ECKANKAR suspected, as I do, that the Temple was itself a causative agent in these vast world changes. Book Two of *The Shariyat-Ki-Sugmad,* the scripture of ECKANKAR, opens with this statement: "In the beginning it is said that the influence of the ECK on world history is and has been enormous; but few other than the ECK Masters and a few chelas have realized this."

1

The main purpose of this book is to show this enormous influence of ECK on world history, using the Temple of ECK as an example. This isn't an eyewitness report of one who was on the Temple building site, for I never set foot within a thousand miles of the Temple until a year after the construction was finished.

My story is a different one. I want to show the impact the building of the Temple of ECK had on those of us who were, outwardly, far away from it. And that includes just about the whole human race! Such stories are perhaps all the more remarkable in illustrating the wide influence of the Temple.

Just as the Temple of ECK has reached out across continents and oceans to encircle us all with its presence, so too shall it reach out across the decades and centuries to embrace distant generations. Who knows? Maybe one day you and I will be there, in another era, gazing back at the ancient history of the twentieth century and marveling at what was started in that momentous year of 1989.

The Prelude

1

A Prophecy Three Times Told

Imagine you are living in the seventeenth century. ECK is still a secret teaching, as it has been for almost five thousand years. The brotherhood of the Vairagi ECK Masters have decided the conditions would soon be right once again to make these teachings known to the public, to bring the teachings of the Light and Sound to the world.

And imagine a meeting had been called by the spiritual hierarchy to discuss the best way to do this. You are sitting in the meeting. What would you suggest? How would it be done?

The first problem that would naturally arise is this: How do you reestablish a credible foundation of truth when the original teachings have had five millennia to get scattered all over the globe, mixed up, lost, confused, and corrupted? Someone is going to have the difficult task of gathering the scattered fragments.

It will take a person who loves to research, study, read, travel, and do a lot of detective work. And where the outer teachings can't be recovered, he will need to be able to go to the Temples of Golden Wisdom on the inner planes and continue the research there. He'll need to have a diverse and complex mind that can see remote connections. He will have to be keenly interested in almost everything, because he'll need to lay a foundation of thought and ideas that will appeal to every temperament and background.

On top of all this, the candidate will have to be a rebel, able to fight the natural resistance that comes from the introduction of any new idea. He'll need to go against the grain and promote himself and his own ideas. There won't be anyone there to clear the way for him.

That's a pretty tall order for one man. But if you put all the needed qualifications together you'd come up with Peddar Zaskq, also known as Paul Twitchell, the man who founded modern-day ECKANKAR.

One of the ECK Masters looks around the table and says, "Fine. We train Peddar Zaskq for the job and send him out there. Supposing he gets as far as gathering the teachings and founding the movement. That's an enormous job, more than enough to occupy the mission of one Living ECK Master. What comes next?"

A second ECK Master stands up to speak to his Vairagi brothers. "I see it this way. We will have to take this mass of spiritual knowledge, for centuries veiled in mystery and archaic traditions, and reshape it into a modern religion accessible to all!"

That is quite another problem and requires a whole other set of skills than the first task. The candidate for this job will need to be able to put the ancient teachings into plain language without diluting their spiritual potency. He will have the great challenge of transforming a small, spiritually revolutionary group into a large, smoothly run religious organization that can meet the spiritual needs of millions of people.

The job would require a person with the imagination to merge an ancient teaching into the mainstream culture of modern times. He will have to build all sorts of bridges to meet the people of the world halfway. Otherwise the teaching will remain just a private little mystery school on the fringes of civilization, doomed to extinction.

Within the context of ECK tradition, his mission will be even more revolutionary than Peddar Zaskq's. Yet at the same time, it will take a man with infinite patience and outstanding organizational skills, for he will have to build a foundation strong enough to last for centuries. Put all of these qualities together and who fits the requirements? Wah Z, Sri Harold Klemp. As the Mahanta, the Living ECK Master, he is the present spiritual leader of ECKANKAR.

Historically the first spiritual revolutionary is usually a thinker, intellectual, and outsider. He must fight the system to introduce his new idea. He attracts to himself people who like this atmosphere. They feel they are changing the world, and they are.

But the time inevitably comes when the movement must be integrated into society. It always takes a different kind of leader to do this. And he often attracts different followers. Many of the early rebels often leave at this time, disillusioned. They see the merging in with society as a capitulation of the old ideals. They are unable to recognize that the real and lasting change begins when their revolution is accepted by the world. So with great pronouncements of disappointment, they drift away. Yet the later movement owes them a great debt. It takes a special breed to create a spiritual revolution.

So imagine yourself now back at the meeting of the ECK Masters. You need two very talented but quite different people to bring ECKANKAR to the world again. But after all they are not so very different. For above all else, they must be dedicated servants of the SUGMAD, or God, and examples to all the world of spiritual Mastership.

I have no idea whether anything like the above meeting ever took place. But it helps to try on the hat of an ECK Master occasionally, to stand back from the whirl of current events and catch the vision.

* * *

Sometimes it takes a long perspective, like that above, to see where the Mahanta is leading ECKANKAR. If one looks only at the moment, he is apt to think that the Living ECK Master is making things up as he goes along. Nothing could be further from the truth.

Some critics have said, "Paul Twitchell got ECKANKAR off to a good start, but then Harold Klemp took it off track and started making it into a religion." This is a view that ignores the long perspective, including Paul Twitchell's long-term perspective. After all, one of the last discourses Paul wrote was titled "ECK as the New Religion of the Age."

There are three remarkable prophecies about the mission of Sri Harold Klemp. Each of them occurred well before he began taking ECKANKAR in its new direction. Each of them beautifully illustrates how that new direction was known well ahead of time. And each of them were given to Sri Harold by the Vairagi Adepts themselves.

The first of the three prophecies is told in Sri Harold's book *Child in the Wilderness*. In chapters 12 through 16 Sri Harold unfolds the dramatic story of how he first experienced God-Realization in April 1970. The whole episode is played out on the stage of a bridge over a river in Wisconsin. Why a bridge? Why not under the tree of enlightenment like Buddha, or a mountaintop like Moses? This setting for one of the most important events in the life of a great spiritual leader was no coincidence. It was the age-old drama of the SUGMAD speaking to ITS creation.

Sri Harold's enlightenment upon the bridge speaks volumes about his mission. He was to take the old method of teaching ECKANKAR across a bridge of consciousness into a whole new area. If one rereads those chapters with this in mind, he will see them in a new light. This is another example of how the Mahanta is the prototype for those who follow him.

Part of the trial of that night of realization on the bridge for Sri Harold was a cold and shocking plunge into the icy waters of the river beneath the bridge. Fifteen years later, when he began taking ECKANKAR across the bridge of consciousness, it would prove to be a shocking plunge for many in ECK. It would unbalance them. And those who trusted totally in the Mahanta would survive the plunge and come out stronger for it.

The second prophetic experience of Sri Harold is described in his book *Soul Travelers of the Far Country* and occurred in November 1978. The ECK Master Fubbi Quantz gave him this prophecy. Sri Harold writes:

> Fubbi Quantz revealed my mission to me on the inner planes, in another dimension of time and space. There he pointed to a water channel (the ECK teachings) that needed cleaning. While scrubbing my section of the channel, I noted that the entire channel was subdivided into a number of well-defined units. Each represented the time frame of a certain Living ECK Master from the past or future.

The water channel was like a plumbing pipe with an elbow joint: The channel made a right-angle turn at the elbow joint.

Fubbi Quantz said that during my term of office the teachings of ECK would be given to people in a wholly new way. A completely new direction would occur during my time. The near future would see a historic turning point in the manner of teaching ECK.[1]

This second prophecy builds naturally on the first. In the first, Sri Harold took the plunge into the river (the ECK), signifying complete surrender to Divine Spirit. He was almost overcome by the shock. In the second prophecy, he is nearing Mastership and is able to work in harmony with the flow of spiritual current, turning the ECK teachings in a totally new direction.

The third prophecy occurred on August 19, 1981, just a few months before he became the next Living ECK Master. Several ECK Masters had met on the inner planes to discuss the passing of the Rod of ECK Power on October 22. As Sri Harold writes in *Soul Travelers of the Far Country:*

> When the meeting came to a close, Dap Ren turned to me and said, 'Come with me on a long journey to the Himalayas.'
>
> Rebazar pointed at the distant peaks and shrugged. 'He's already been to the Katsupari Monastery and Agam Des. Why not something new?'
>
> The ECK-Vidya was giving insight into my spiritual mission. Dap Ren's invitation was to go to old places, places well familiar in our travels. Rebazar was saying that the missions of Peddar Zaskq and Dap Ren had explored these areas. I was to bring the high ECK teachings down into

10

the everyday lives of people. So our journey was to the lowlands by the seashore.

The lowlands had a greater population because life was easier there than in the forbidding mountains. Only a few hardy travelers had the stamina necessary for survival in the wilds. This was therefore the ECK-Vidya restating a part of my mission to come.[2]

Thus, long before he began taking ECKANKAR in a new direction, Sri Harold had been given three lucid descriptions of his mission to come: Across a bridge into a new consciousness, in a right-angle turn from past methods of presenting ECK, and down from the isolated mountaintops to the valley where the people live. It would have been a foolhardy and reckless mistake for him to have ignored these prophecies.

Yet when he slowly and gently began helping us across the bridge, some people began to complain and left ECK. When he started to lead us down off the mountain and asked us to mingle with the world, more critics emerged and left in a huff. When he started moving the ECK teachings in a new direction, even more people became upset.

Yet for each person who couldn't or didn't want to follow where the Mahanta was leading, there were many who did and were grateful for it. For they recognized that it wasn't an ECK Master named Harold Klemp who was behind the changes, it was the ECK Itself. And they recognized that ECKANKAR would be better for it. The little spiritual revolution started by Paul Twitchell was ready to move out into the world and become a part of civilization.

On Thursday, October 22, 1981, Sri Harold Klemp accepted the Rod of ECK Power and became the Mahanta, the Living ECK Master. Later he would write, "The acceptance of the Rod of ECK Power is an initiation where instructions come directly from the Source of Life ITSELF. Henceforth the will of the SUGMAD determines the new Living ECK Master's actions on a grand scale. This rite is the marriage of the macrocosm and microcosm in him."[3]

And "Each Godman brings to earth a unique talent with which to give Soul the eternal message of ECK in the most expedient manner."[4]

Whenever the Rod of ECK Power is passed, there is a revitalization throughout all the God Worlds. On earth it may be a subtle shift, noticed by only a few. The struggle for ECK Mastership was now behind him. But Sri Harold faced the new struggle of rescuing ECKANKAR from an impending crisis. It would be an awesome task. Could this gentle, soft-spoken Master do it? Could he turn ECKANKAR around and set it in the new direction which was willed by the SUGMAD ITSELF? I imagine there were some who wondered, even among the Vairagi.

2

A Vision of the Mahanta's Mission

On October 22, 1981, Sri Harold Klemp became the Mahanta, the Living ECK Master. On October 22, 1990, one of the most significant days in the spiritual history of planet earth, he dedicated the Temple of ECK. Those nine astounding years saw ECKANKAR and the world change dramatically.

I was asked to give a talk at an ECKANKAR retreat in spring 1991. The title of the talk was "A Vision of the Mahanta's Mission." To prepare for the talk, I reviewed all the information I had about what Sri Harold had written and done over the decade of the 1980s. I was trying to catch the vision of what he was doing, trying to discover the framework of how it all fit together.

One night, while sitting with piles of notes before me on the table, an inspiration came to me. Why not organize the material in nine stages, like the first nine planes of the God Worlds of ECK or the nine steps of the ziggurat roof on the new Temple of ECK? When I did this, all my notes seemed to fall into a very natural order.

This is how I presented the talk. Many in the audience came up to me later and said the presentation really helped them catch the vision of the Mahanta's mission.

The intent of this chapter is to sketch in the broad view of what I feel the Mahanta was doing in the first nine years of his mission. It will give depth and background to the Dream Weaver chronicles which follow. I will call this year-by-year unfolding of the Mahanta's mission the nine-year plan.

The successful execution of this ambitious plan stands as a true and divine miracle. The ECK Master Paul Twitchell once said, "A miracle is a changed consciousness." The change in consciousness which Sri Harold and the spiritual hierarchy helped us establish is global in its breadth and divine in its reach.

* * *

Year 1: October 22, 1981, to October 22, 1982. "A Quiet Beginning"

In 1980, Harold Klemp was the candidate to become the next Living ECK Master. The task before him was an awesome one. The full force of the mission was so great, at first he found it difficult to handle. In his first talk as the new Living ECK Master in October 1981, he said: "The time had come last year when I was approached by the Living ECK Master; by the Order of the Vairagi; and by the Silent Ones, the Council of the Nine. I was asked if I would take this position, and of course I said yes, because I felt strong enough. . . .

"When I said yes, it knocked me for a loop and I went flipping over backwards a couple of times. . . .

"There was a meeting up in the Himalayan mountains last year [1980] where the ECK Masters Fubbi Quantz, Rebazar Tarzs, Lai Tsi, Gopal Das, Peddar

Zaskq, and others were walking along this dirt road, and I was with them. They looked over the situation, and they were very... understanding... and let me off the hook for another year."[1]

Yet already, Sri Harold knew the direction of his mission. In January 1980 he had received his vision of the site for the Temple of ECK.[2] The spiritual currents were surging strongly, and it took extraordinary stamina to work with them.

When Sri Harold accepted the mantle of the Living ECK Master on October 22, 1981, ECKANKAR was launched into a new era. But at the time, it wasn't apparent.

For all the force behind this Mahanta's mission, the beginning was deceptively quiet. No grand announcements came forth. No startling changes of policy or direction. Eighth Initiate Millie Moore recalls her puzzlement over this: "When Harold took the Rod of ECK Power in 1981, I said, 'Oh boy! My beloved ECK is in good hands; now I can relax. Surely everything will get straightened out in a hurry!'

"But at first it appeared that nothing happened."[3]

For a Master whose biography was titled *The Wind of Change,* there didn't even seem to be a stirring breeze. Millie continues: "For two years he quietly left us to ourselves to go within, to find the Mahanta for ourselves. . . . For many of us, it was a major crossroad. The movement of ECKANKAR was taking a new direction."[4]

Reading between the lines in Millie's comments, I believe that she thought ECKANKAR was in need of a new and clear direction. Through the seventies, although ECKANKAR had appeared to grow, it was in dire need of a clear vision of where it was going and how it would get there.

Inwardly, the first of the nine steps in the plan was being constructed. Sri Harold knew he had to take the teachings of ECK in a whole new direction. Not just a direction different than the founding of modern-day ECKANKAR in 1965, but a new direction relative to millennia of tradition.

For almost five thousand years ECK had been a secret teaching. It had been forced into this role to survive. The religious persecutions in ancient times were not so mild as nowadays. To teach ECK openly meant torture and death. But making a virtue out of necessity, many present-day ECKists viewed the cloak of secrecy and mystery as the essence of the ECK teachings.

Paul Twitchell had brought the teachings back out into the open again. But the inertia of the secret-teaching tradition followed right behind, surrounding ECKANKAR in an aura of mystery for the public at large.

This didn't mean ECKANKAR would no longer have an esoteric, or hidden, side to it. But Sri Harold's mission was to establish ECKANKAR as a mainstream, global religion. He knew this would be a shock to many. Sri Harold writes: "My object was to make the necessary changes slowly. It was enough of a trauma for many ECKists to reexamine their loyalties. . . . In other words, were they following the ECK or the personality of a Master?"[5]

Thus for ECKANKAR, step one of the Mahanta's nine-year plan closely resembled the experience of a First Initiate in ECK. It was a time to get oriented. A time to go quietly within, to sense the new direction, to reexamine one's goals and motives. There was a need for the movement to go back to its basics, to review the steps to God, to recall the original goals of the path of ECK.

That the approach began to work very quickly is revealed by Sri Harold in a March–April 1982 communication to the initiates: "There is an awakening occurring among the Initiates of ECK that it really is possible to reach Self-Realization and God-Realization, and to realize the Kingdom of Heaven while still living in the body."

"The initiates are realizing, often *for the first time,* [italics mine] that it is possible to reach their former goals."[6]

* * *

Year 2: October 22, 1982, to October 22, 1983. "The Wind of Change"

As ECKANKAR passed into year two of the nine-year plan, the inner mission of the Mahanta shifted up a plane, to the Astral, or emotional level. A lot of housecleaning needed to be done there. Behind the scenes and unknown to most of the membership, a battle was brewing. Although the Rod of ECK Power had been passed to Sri Harold, the former Living ECK Master, Darwin Gross, had trouble accepting the transition.

The inevitable consequence of this was a deep emotional strain within the body of ECK initiates. But the ECK waits for no man. One must either flow with Divine Spirit or be left behind. As Sri Harold wrote, "The teacher of detachment had become attached. He did not want to let go the reins of his old job. This illustrates perfection is an ongoing quest, even for those high in the spiritual hierarchy."[7]

He continued, "Gross's failure to understand attachment versus SUGMAD's will precipitated the spiritual crisis that led to his dismissal from the Vairagi

17

Order in late 1983. It remains one of the saddest chapters in the contemporary history of ECKANKAR."[8]

Sri Harold had given the chelas a year to go within and rediscover their spiritual direction. Now, the testing time was to begin. The age-old struggle of the opposites on the Astral Plane emerged into the collective consciousness of ECKANKAR. Many thought they had evolved far beyond the trials and storms of the emotions, only to be caught by surprise.

"This attachment to a personality," Sri Harold explains, "is a recurring reality that confronts every new Living ECK Master. A certain portion of people in ECK cling doggedly to the personality of a Master because they do not see the ECK behind all he does. They try to make him out to be a god, which is contrary to the ECK principle of the Living Word."[9]

The Wind of Change began to blow. The winds of 1983 would prove to be just the front of a raging storm that was about to shake the movement.

* * *

Year 3: October 22, 1983, to October 22 1984. "Storms of Trial"

Year three of the nine-year plan saw a shift into the Causal Plane. Here the full force of past misdeeds return to the sender. The Causal Plane is the plane where cause and effect hold sway, and there is no escaping the consequences of one's actions. This year in ECKANKAR was a graphic display of the process in action.

The time of quiet inner reflection was over. It was time to act, to decide, and to take the consequences that came with the decision. The ECK, Divine Spirit, was giving each and every one of Its followers the choice of which road to take. At the Causal Plane initiation, the seeker must choose between the right-hand path, the left-hand path, or the middle path of ECK. Some were able to easily follow the middle path and move through this period gracefully. Others stood at the crossroads and trembled.

Sri Harold wrote: "ECKANKAR is here to stay. Born in controversy, its future points to more rocky ground ahead. . . . A crisis is an opportunity in disguise. A solution is hidden in the folds of every reverse. . . .

"Storms are yet to rage; the clouds of greater ones lurk on the horizon. Each tempest will try to put an overpowering fear into your heart, in order to scare you onto some detour to God."[10]

ECKANKAR was going through a severe crisis. And many of the chelas passed through the classic five stages of grieving which Dr. Elisabeth Kübler-Ross has described.[11] These are stages a person often goes through when they face a great loss.

The first stage is denial. ("It couldn't really happen in ECKANKAR! I don't believe it. There must be some mistake.") The truth seems too painful to bear.

The second stage is anger. ("Who is responsible? This shouldn't be happening!") The main effort at this stage is to assign blame. And plenty of finger pointing was going on in ECKANKAR during this stage.

The third stage is bargaining. ("OK, it is true. But surely we can resolve all these differences. Let's all sit down together, forget the past, and find a comfortable solution.") Here the person is standing at the fork in the road. It is easier to talk and discuss endlessly than to make the decision as to which way to go.

The fourth stage is depression, a sense of hopelessness. ("Woe is me. My life is dashed to pieces, and my faith is gone. I have nothing left to live for.") This can

19

be a long and painful experience. It is the last retreat. Either the person regains courage and faith or steps off the path in total discouragement.

The last stage is acceptance. One faces the truth and deals with it. ("Where do we go from here? Let's pick up the pieces and move on.")

Some of these stages took several years for people to work through. There was often a wavering back and forth between the different stages. But meanwhile, the Mahanta was rolling up his sleeves and looking to the future. The ECK ever moves on, pushing forward into new spiritual frontiers.

"A slow but steady building program is under way on all fronts in ECKANKAR," Sri Harold said to the initiates. "I want to go slowly with each project and build well rather than hurry and build on sand. There will be plenty of work for each of you."[12]

The Causal Plane is the place to plant seeds for the future. On that plane one works with the law of threes. That year Sri Harold planted three important seeds which would emerge in future years as pillars of the new ECKANKAR organization:

1. A seed for the future ECK Writer's Group. "A number of good writers will emerge from among the initiates in ECK. They will become the master writers who will carry the news of the Divine Spirit to places where people are ready for it."[13]

2. A seed for the future field organization. "Eventually, I expect to see a definite system of field organization that is modeled after the spiritual hierarchy's."[14]

3. A seed for the future Vahana, or missionary, work. "Often as I sit at the typewriter to write to you, it strikes me as an awesome thing to

think of all the countries where the ECK has put you in Its service. Bitter political enmity divides the leaders of nations, but a cohesive bond prevents the world from falling apart despite this: the quiet work you do to bring the practices of the Light and Sound of ECK to these jumbled times."[15]

Sri Harold proceeded to set in motion the next step of his mission. Having planted the seeds, it was time to shift up another plane.

* * *

Year 4: October 22, 1984, to October 22, 1985. "Closing the Chapter on an Era"

In year four of the nine-year plan I saw the focus of the Mahanta's mission shift to the Mental Plane. It is the last of the lower worlds, a plane where old business is wrapped up and preparations are made for the spiritual move up into the pure positive God Worlds. And so it went for ECKANKAR. This would be the movement's last full year with its headquarters in California.

As the dark storm clouds of 1984 began to clear, the Mahanta began to speak of the coming sunshine of a new golden age. "Only the Mahanta, the Living ECK Master, has the ability to stop the downhill fall of today's spiritual decline. He is the sole agent with the spiritual power to establish a new golden age."[16]

This ray of hope after ECKANKAR's Dark Night of Soul brought in a burst of fresh optimism. But what is the essential factor in a golden age? The secret lies in the Golden, or loving, Heart. Many members were weary, eager to put the past behind them. More than anything, they needed to reopen their hearts. Sri Harold wrote in 1985: "The closer one gets to the Ocean of

Love and Mercy, the more he is the Golden Heart. His love for the SUGMAD outshines any concern for the welfare of his little self."[17]

With the theme of the Golden Heart and a golden age, ECKANKAR began to find itself again. Even the world responded to the optimism. As Millie Moore put it, "Before—not just in the ECKANKAR world but throughout the world at large—everybody was talking about doomsday, the end of the world. Now we're talking about the new Golden Age of ECKANKAR.

"That was the year everybody started wearing golden hearts."[18]

But the Mahanta's plan was just beginning. In 1985 he wrote: "This is an exciting time, but the real building of the ECK foundation is still to come. The ECK is the Wind of Change, and change is the ingredient that makes life the dynamic thing that it is."[19]

ECKANKAR was ready to put the past and the lower worlds behind it.

* * *

Year 5: October 22, 1985, to October 22, 1986. "The Year of Spiritual Healing"

The transition from the Fourth to the Fifth, or Soul, Plane is a giant spiritual move up. It is the time when Soul finally arrives home in the pure spiritual worlds from whence It came. Its vagabond wanderings are over, as It establishes Itself in the bosom of Divine Spirit.

And so in 1986, the fifth year of the nine-year plan, it appeared the Mahanta shifted the focus of his mission up to the Soul Plane. This would be the year the ECKANKAR International Office would move to Minneapolis and begin to finally establish a home for ECKANKAR.

I feel this year marked the real beginning of Sri Harold's mission. This was also the year that he began giving titles or themes to each year. "The Year of Spiritual Healing" was the theme chosen for this first year in the worlds of Spirit.

Sri Harold said in 1986, "The move of the ECK Office to Minnesota marks the beginning of a new era, and it has been hard-won.

"The move was a spiritual move. Whatever happens out here is just a reflection of something that has already happened on the inner."[20]

The Year of Spiritual Healing was a natural beginning point for the new cycle. The members of ECK had a lot of healing to do. The rugged journey through the lower worlds had left a lot of sore wounds.

When an individual reaches the Soul Plane in his unfoldment, it marks the stage of his spiritual liberation. I saw a remarkable waking dream that expressed this theme of liberation at the time of ECKANKAR's move. As the caravan of ECKANKAR moving vans rolled into Minneapolis in early July 1986, America was having a gala celebration for the one hundredth birthday of the Statue of Liberty. Like ECKANKAR, the statue had been completely renewed over the previous few years in preparation for the celebration.

In future chapters of this book, we will see how the theme of liberation sweeps the world whenever the Mahanta takes a big step forward with his mission. The waking dream of the Statue of Liberty would prove to be the first of many I would see surrounding the Mahanta's mission. Another quote from Millie Moore fits in here. She writes, "The funny part is that people don't give the Master credit for these things. We forget that this Mahanta is not ours. He belongs to the world."[21]

In the spring of 1986, Sri Harold related a conversation he had with the great ECK Master Rebazar Tarzs. "Can a chela ever know the unconditional love of the Mahanta for him?" Sri Harold asked Rebazar.

" 'He can,' said the Tibetan, 'But only when he turns everything over to the Mahanta—all hopes, dreams, fears, and desires. The tears of Soul lead to a deep and final cleansing which brings upliftment and release, spiritual liberation.' "[22]

Until the ECK, Divine Spirit, touches the heart with the Sound and Light of God, there is virtually no lasting progress on Soul's homeward journey. The Year of Spiritual Healing reached deep into the hearts of thousands. Writes Millie, "The Year of Spiritual Healing was a major earthquake in consciousness. Healings began to take place. . . . There was a sharing, a welcoming, and an opening of our hearts to the loved ones coming into ECK."[23]

As people looked around, they began to realize the miracle Sri Harold had accomplished. ECKANKAR had been renewed, reborn, transformed, and uplifted. Yet for all of that, Sri Harold pressed on with his mission. He had a clear vision of the SUGMAD's will and where it would lead.

* * *

Year 6: October 22, 1986, to October 22, 1987. "The Year of the Arahata"

Now that the movement had a firm home base and was on its way to being healed, the next phase of the Master's plan moved into action. ECKANKAR had been self-absorbed for the past several years, and it was now time to turn to the world again. The first phase of this process would be the Year of the Arahata, the ECK teacher.

"It's been a very good year," wrote Sri Harold. "The Year of Spiritual Healing began on October 22, 1985, and its force will continue into the foreseeable future, blending smoothly into the Year of the Arahata, which began on October 22, 1986. Each year melts into the next, and the power of each is added to future years."[24]

Why is the teacher so important? Sri Harold writes, "The future of ECKANKAR is mainly with the Arahata. Our teaching methods can inspire people on the path of Sound and Light. It is essentially our approach of telling stories with spiritual principles that will reach the people."[25]

Following our analogy of relating the Mahanta's mission to the God Worlds of ECK, the Year of the Arahata marks a shift in the nine-year plan, up to the Sixth Plane. Now it appeared that the real goal of the plan was coming into sight—the Ninth Plane, or ninth step, where the mission becomes service to all life. But the plan must be unfolded gradually.

Sri Harold writes in summer 1987: "I am going step-by-step with the whole movement of ECK. First, attention is on Soul Travel; then, more on the Light and Sound; finally, on the love of service to God for ITS sake alone."[26]

The Year of the Arahata saw some minor changes in ECKANKAR. But the movement seemed at last to be settling down again. People were catching their breath after the move to Minnesota and making adjustments to the new consciousness which came with it.

Then Sri Harold came out with yet another call to prepare for further changes. He had started slowly, but once he got started, the change was almost continuous. In fall 1987 Sri Harold wrote: "The future will see any number of earthshaking moments of truth we will have to face.

"Every time we think that we just about have the ECK program in hand, a major shift occurs that makes us look at our spiritual loyalties from a new angle."[27]

Of course everyone wondered, What next?

* * *

Year 7: October 22, 1987, to October 22, 1988. "The Year of the Shariyat"

The Mahanta's mission shifts to the Seventh Plane. The higher vibrations poured out into the world, keeping up the pressure of change. Sri Harold once again sent out a call of preparedness. If anyone had any doubts where the Mahanta was taking ECKANKAR, these doubts should have been erased that year. In spring 1988, Sri Harold wrote:

> We are coming into a notably rugged season of testing. Tomorrow will show new ways in which the Mahanta will deliver news of ECK to people of the world. . . .
>
> The mission of the current Mahanta, the Living ECK Master is to make the ECK message available to the nations of all people. Since human beings are at all levels of consciousness, he introduces the teachings in dozens of ways.
>
> The global reach of his mission clashes with all who have a one-track state of mind.[28]

What were these tests? The first big test concerned the word *religion*. For most of the first twenty years of ECKANKAR, some of its members said that it wasn't a religion. The subtitle under ECKANKAR kept changing. It went from "ECKANKAR, the Ancient Science of Soul Travel," to "ECKANKAR, the Path of Total Awareness," to "ECKANKAR, a

26

Way of Life," then back to "ECKANKAR, the Ancient Science of Soul Travel" again.

It seemed to me that part of the problem was an attempt to be one thing and appear as another. ECKANKAR had all the elements of a religion, yet some didn't want to call it that. Finally Sri Harold broke through this attitude. In a humorous comparison he wrote:

> Some came into ECKANKAR with the mistaken belief that it was not a religion. It has a God, a Holy Spirit, a Master, a bible, many temples, and a host of spiritual travelers to administer creation. There is a saying: If it looks like a duck, walks like a duck, quacks like a duck—it is a duck. The same is true of ECKANKAR as a religion. It has all the earmarks of a religion. But that is only its outer form. Those who criticize the label forget that the quintessence of the ECK teachings is its inner side.[29]

Sri Harold had been right in his prediction that this new label would stick in the throats of some ECKists. More than a few refused to go this far. As the new subtitle under ECKANKAR became "the New-Age Religion," they called it quits.

I imagine Sri Harold put in the "New-Age" part of the subtitle as a transition phrase to lessen the shock to people. At least they could say it was a new-age religion, and not an orthodox one. But after a year or two, the subtitle was changed to the more direct "Religion of the Light and Sound of God."

A second big test followed on the heels of the first. At the 1988 ECK Springtime Seminar in Anaheim, California, Sri Harold announced the opening of HU Chants to the uninitiated. These HU Chant gatherings had been special times for many ECKists to get together and just be with each other. When Sri Harold opened these to the public, it upset some members. And the following year when he explained the ECK Worship Service, that upset some even more, especially those still grappling with the word *religion*.

In the chapter on the global initiation, we will see how the gift of HU to the public fits the master plan in a very special way.

The First Year of the Shariyat and the following year, titled the Second Year of the Shariyat, helped prepare for the coming of a new Temple of Golden Wisdom. A main purpose of these temples is the housing and teaching of the sacred works of ECKANKAR, the many volumes of the Shariyat-Ki-Sugmad. These are the holy books of ECK.

Building a Temple of Golden Wisdom on the physical plane, right on the doorstep of humanity, would be the ultimate act of making the secret teachings public once again. It was necessary to prepare the world for this extraordinary adventure by first sharing the HU and focusing on the Shariyat.

To quote Millie Moore one more time: "All the while, you see the whole Master Plan carefully and quietly falling into place.

"I thought, What a beautiful Master Plan. It's a groundwork that will last for centuries!"[30]

I'm not so sure it fell *quietly* into place! From where I stood, it sounded as loud as a tornado. But the plan was indeed falling into place. At the end of the First Year of the Shariyat, Sri Harold wrote: "A shift in spiritual direction is taking place. It is a transition from, What is the *form* of ECKANKAR? to, What is its *substance?* . . . This new age of spirituality might well be called 'The Sharing of God.' . . . ECKANKAR is growing up. We are discovering better ways to share our knowledge of ECK with grace and love."[31]

*   *   *

The eighth and ninth years of the nine-year plan concern the building of the Temple of ECK and its extraordinary impact on the world. (These years will be covered later in this book.) At the end of the ninth year of the nine-year plan, named the Year of the HU, Sri Harold dedicated the Temple of ECK, a gift to the world. At that moment, his mission had reached the top of the Ninth Plane and touched the Tenth, the plane of the HU. A Niagara Falls of Light and Sound came pouring into the Temple.

Part one of the Mahanta's mission was complete. He had taken his mission to the top of the spiritual mountain. Now part two would begin.

And what was that? To take the teachings of ECKANKAR to the whole world. The first year of this second part was titled, appropriately, the Year of the Vahana. A *Vahana* is one who carries the Light and Sound of God to others. ECKANKAR was now poised to move out into the world, in service to all.

The Chronicles

3

Vision Quest One
On Sacred Ground

The Mahanta, the Living ECK Master is the prototype of the age for those who follow him. He is
the main vehicle of the ECK, the foremost pioneer into
God's vast domain. He blazes the trail, that those who
follow will find their way prepared.

In January 1980 Sri Harold had a vision of the site
for the future Temple of ECK. His vision established
an anchor point in the inner worlds for what would
later emerge on the physical plane.

Initiates in ECK who are aligned with the goals
and plans of the spiritual hierarchy often pick up on
these plans before they are made manifest. Sometimes
we are quick to conclude that our ideas and inspira-
tions are of our own creation. Later we recognize that
they were seeds planted by the Mahanta, as part of
a long-range goal which may yet be years away.

So it was that six months after Sri Harold's prototype vision, I had one of my own. Though I couldn't
have known it at the time, it was a vision that would
evolve over the next ten years and connect with the
events surrounding the building and dedication of the
Temple.

The vision came in a dream. I awoke in the inner worlds, somewhere in a primeval forest. The moon above floated in and out of wispy clouds and cast eerie shadows on the forest floor. I stood in hushed reverence, awed by the immensity of the aged trees and the silence of the night. I was naked, except for a deerskin loincloth. My red skin was that of a Native American.

I was on a vision quest—a lonely vigil of fasting, worship, and prayer out in the wilderness, in hopes the Great Spirit, or ECK, would grant me a revelation. Surrounding me was the great forest that used to stretch across the North American continent from the Great Plains all the way to the eastern seaboard.

For days I had been wandering the forest, and the fatigue was beginning to wear me down. I moved ahead, pushing my way through the underbrush. Suddenly I broke out of the thick brush into a large circular clearing. A deep mystery brooded over the area. I knew instantly that this was the place I had been searching for. Once I stepped inside that circle, I would be entering a different world.

Fear of the unknown gripped me. Would I die? Or would the Great Spirit grant me a vision? With heart pounding, I stepped forward into the circle. At that moment I turned into a golden eagle and soared skyward in a burst of ecstatic freedom.

Winging high up over my new domain, I felt the exhilaration of a liberation I'd never known. Though in eagle's form, my thoughts were lucid and human: So this is how it feels to be an eagle! To encounter an eagle in a vision was considered very fortunate by most of the Native American tribes. But to become the eagle—this marked the vision as one to be shared. It meant the site of the vision had been blessed with great spiritual power and was sacred ground.

Time passed, and I felt a need to descend from the sky back to the clearing. I glided down and alighted before a stone, returning to the form of an Indian. I knelt before the stone and made of it an altar. A profound humbleness came over me, tinted with the sadness of a long-lost heart. Somehow I knew the vision was not yet complete. I prayed to the Great Spirit to lead me where It would.

As I prayed, a strange glow began to surround me. I looked up and saw a pillar of bluish white light descending from the heavens. Slowly it came down, ever so slowly, until its base touched the stone altar and its upper part extended skyward, beyond the range of my sight. Then a sphere of the purest and softest light started coming down the shaft, again, ever so slowly.

When the sphere of light finally descended all the way to the altar, it changed into a beautiful white owl. Its eyes were soft and glistening with purity and wisdom. It spoke in a human voice. Its words were a sonorous melody of piercing beauty and penetrated straight to the core of my heart. It spoke of ancient times and of ages yet to come. Its prophecies were poetry; its words a melody. Then the shining bird fell silent.

Its form dissolved into the sphere of light, and slowly it ascended the shining pillar, the pillar withdrawing with the sphere. Soon, all was silence and darkness again. I remained kneeling quietly for a few minutes.

I awoke from the dream and looked at the clock. It was 4:00 a.m. The date was July 12.

I would later realize that this was my first experience connected with the Temple of ECK. The spiritual vortex had already been established and made operative by Sri Harold's vision. My vision was spawned by his.

35

As I lay in bed, pondering on my dream, a number of questions arose in my mind. Why did the Light and Sound of God come to me in this form? At the time, I had no knowledge of or interest in Native American traditions. I felt this sacred ground existed somewhere in the United States. But where? Why had I dreamed about it? And why was I an Indian?

The ECK communicates to people in many forms. To the Native Americans It often spoke through animals. Because of its ability to see in darkness and its watchfulness, the owl has been associated with clairvoyance and prophecy.[1]

Later, as I studied the traditions of the Native Americans, I came to better understand the meaning and purpose of a vision quest. The seeker would leave the comfort of his familiar social life and trek alone into the remote wilderness. There he was to fast and pray for spiritual guidance. He would seek a vision of his mission and purpose in life.

But more importantly, he sought the gifts of Divine Spirit so he could bring them back and share them with his tribe. On his lonely quest, the seeker would go through a great trial of loneliness, hunger, danger, and silence. From this experience, he would emerge a changed person. The vision quest is one form of the symbolic death and rebirth experience which most spiritual disciplines find necessary for true spiritual understanding.

Yet the vision granted is not the conclusion of a search. It is a beginning. The seeker must return again and again to the inner world of Divine Spirit, seeking further clarification, guidance, and inspiration. He must struggle to make his vision of practical value in his life by serving others. Quite often, the animal that appears in the vision becomes a special companion throughout the person's life. It appears at key moments to bring warning, prophecies, or revelations.

Many people in the West have looked beyond their own borders for a sacred ground or holy land. If Christian or Jew or Moslem, they looked to the Middle East. Others looked to India or the mountains of Tibet as the place to go on a pilgrimage.

The Temple of ECK is the first modern Temple of Golden Wisdom and is home for the teachings of ECKANKAR. I feel that part of the reason my dream came to me in the form of a Native American vision quest, drawing on my past-life experience as a Native American, was so I would better appreciate the significance of this Golden Wisdom Temple—that it was sacred ground.

* * *

A year after this dream, in July 1981, a business trip took me to the northeastern part of the United States. As my flight headed north on the night of July 4, I could see the fireworks of Independence Day celebrations. This rare bird's-eye spectacle seemed to me to promise a special trip.

After a week of training and classes, I was glad to rent a car and get out into the countryside. I just followed the country roads wherever they went, taking time to hike among the trees and along the streams. Around dusk I came to a lonely stretch of road in a maple forest. Pulling over to the side of the road, I turned off the engine and got out to just savor the moment.

A wonderful quiet had settled over the forest. I took a deep breath of the summer-scented air and listened to the gentle breeze rustle the treetops.

Suddenly a giant brown shape came rushing toward me out of the dusk. I was about to dive for cover when it turned its wings and alighted on a branch not three feet above my head. It was a great horned owl. He just stared at me, and I stared back. After a few moments, he cocked his head, leaned down a little, and gave a long "Whooooooooooo." Then, as if his message was delivered, he flashed his wings and glided off into the trees.

It took me a little while to recover from this delightful surprise. This species of owl is not known for its cozy sociability. It prefers to keep its distance from people.

The recollection of my owl dream drifted into my thoughts. Then it hit me. This was July 12. It was exactly one year earlier, on July 12, 1980, that the vision-quest owl had appeared to me! Here I was, as in my dream, far from home, standing in a remote northern forest, being visited by an owl.

This experience seemed to be a continuation and unfoldment of the original dream. I had left for this trip on America's Independence Day. The fireworks seen from the airplane had been for me a symbol or waking dream of liberation and freedom. This was a variation of my earlier vision, where the eagle was an expression of liberation and freedom.

The link to American independence suggested this chain of events was of more than personal interest. In chapter 2 we saw that when ECKANKAR moved to Minnesota in early July 1986, America was having a grand celebration and fireworks for the one-hundredth birthday of the Statue of Liberty.

The Dream Weaver was starting his tapestry; he was laying out his multicolored threads. Who is the Dream Weaver? He is one of the many faces of the

Mahanta, the Living ECK Master. And he is a Master of his craft.

The owl symbol began to appear more frequently. When it came in a dream, it gave prophecies. When it came in the physical, it was at turning points in my life. I wish to give a few examples before leaving this chapter. I believe the spiritual connection between people and animals is something that has been largely forgotten in our modern urban life.

The night I gave my wife-to-be an engagement ring, a white owl flew right between us, the moment after I put the ring on her finger! This occurred in the downtown area of a large city. My fiancée was so startled by this, she couldn't believe it. "It was just a seagull," she said. "No, I saw it. It was an owl." We had a friendly argument about it while we walked back to her apartment.

When we got there, she said, "Oh never mind. Let's see what's on TV." She flipped on the television. A nature program was just starting. The title of the program was "The Mating Habits of Snowy Owls." "OK," she relented, "So it was an owl!"

Another incident occurred the night our first daughter was born. When the labor pains started, I rushed my wife to the hospital. A white owl flew up to our car just as we drove into the hospital parking lot. Many more examples could be given.

This thread of my story will reappear in a later chapter titled "Vision Quest Two: The Holy Fire of ECK," where the waking-dream theme ties in again with the Temple of ECK.

4

The Bridge of Purification

The waking dream is usually an outer experience given by the Mahanta. Its purpose is to point to a spiritual lesson through an example in your outer life.

The Golden-tongued Wisdom is the voice of the Mahanta that jumps out to impart spiritual insight. It might come through words spoken by another person in a golden moment.[1]

—Sri Harold Klemp

Throughout 1988 and continuing into 1989, a series of recurring dreams had come to me, and I hadn't been able to fathom them. Each dream in the series was similar. I was trying to get home and had to cross a bridge to get there. Some sort of obstacle would get in my way. As I tried to figure a way around or through the obstacle, a woman would come to my aid. Her name would be Kathy, Katherine, Katrina, Kate, or any other similar variation of that popular given name.

But the dreams were not merely repetitions. Each dream would advance me one bridge closer to "home," wherever that was. In early March of 1989, the dream series climaxed in an unexpected way.

In the dream, I found myself in an old, majestic monastery in Italy. Following an inner nudge, I started climbing flights of stairs to reach the very top of the building. After a long climb, I finally reached a little room on the roof, with a panoramic view of the country-side.

In the room stood a woman whose aura radiated strength and peace. "Welcome," she said softly, "I am Catherine of Sienna." This was the famous mystic that had such an influence on fourteenth-century Italy! She reached out and handed me a pair of white cotton gloves. "Do you know what the name *Catherine* means?" she asked me.

"I think it means to purge or cleanse," I said. She smiled. "It simply means purity.[2] Let these white gloves remind you to strive for purity. It is easy to be pure in a monastery. You discovered that in a past life here in Italy, when you sought God through the monastic life. But to find purity while living out in the world, that is the challenge!

"You wish to go home. Only the Mahanta, the Living ECK Master can lead you there. You have many bridges yet to cross. God be with you."

This dream helped put in perspective the whole series on bridges and Kathys. The puzzle pieces were beginning to fit into place. The Dream Weaver was picking up a thread from a past life and weaving it into the present one. I have always had a yearning to live in a monastery, yet I knew instinctively there would be no spiritual growth for me there.

Paul Twitchell wrote a beautiful chapter on purity in his book *Stranger by the River*. The chapter opens with the seeker asking of his teacher, "What is purity, Sire?" Rebazar Tarzs answers, "Purity is the truth of Soul dwelling in God, my son. . . . When man purifies his consciousness, then he begins to walk the path of God in a straightforward manner via the path of ECK."[3]

And later in the dialogue, Rebazar says, "Purity calls for the highest within man. You cannot slander nor can you see the evil in others. If you look for the good in those around thee, then you will bring out the good within them, and make thy neighbor manifest his good qualities."[4]

How is one to develop purity? The Master explains to the seeker, "To become pure you must do three things: first, chant the holy names of God constantly upon thy lips; secondly, do everything in the name of the SUGMAD, thy Father; and third, love the SUGMAD with all thy passion, and also thy neighbor. These three spiritual practices will make thee pure, my son."[5]

About a week after the monastery dream, the imagery shifted out of the dream world into the physical world. One of my college classes was a business course in managerial accounting. The instructor paired us for team projects so we could put into practice what we were studying. I was paired with a student named Kathy Bridges. Her name was a synthesis of the Katherine-and-the-bridge themes I had been dreaming about!

The Katherine-and-the-bridge theme would soon prove to be tied to the Mahanta in an unexpected way.

The 1989 ECK Springtime Seminar was to be held in San Diego, California, on March 24–26. It had been three years since I'd been able to attend a major ECKANKAR seminar, and I was eager to go. Sri Harold once said that whenever you go to a seminar watch everything that happens, for it is really a spiritual journey. Anything that happens on this journey, from the time you leave home until the time you return, contains a spiritual message and opportunity for spiritual growth.

The drive to the airport to catch my flight to San Diego took about an hour. The first thing that caught my attention as I pulled out onto the freeway was a bumper sticker on a car which read "I love Germany!" That's an odd spiritual message, I thought. What in the world could Germany have to do with this journey?

When I got to the very small airport in Eugene, Oregon, I went to check my bags. There was a long line of people at the counter ahead of me. They were a group of German tourists who were on their way home! I thought, Maybe I better start jotting some of this down in my journal.

These two initial images relating to Germany proved to be the first in a series of about ten that came that weekend. In rare instances, I had experienced strings of four or five waking dreams in a row that related to a single theme. But ten was simply beyond belief. Even though I was a believer in how the ECK, Divine Spirit, could arrange physical reality to make a point, this series of waking dreams put me in awe of how It worked.

I felt that the more waking dreams in a series, the more important was the spiritual message. So I knew that something of earthshaking significance was in the air and that it related to Germany and to the Mahanta's mission. But what could it possibly be?

A second theme emerged on my flight to San Diego. I sat next to an American businessman of Chinese descent. We began talking, and he told me he was on his way to Beijing, China. He said he traveled to China several times a year and had gotten to know the nation and people there pretty well.

I asked him whether he thought the Chinese rulers would ever loosen their control over the people and allow a little democratic freedom. His answer was prophetic. He said there was a growing hunger for freedom among the people. He felt a popular uprising could happen, if all the people united.

These waking dreams of Germany and China held personal significance for me. In the early 1980s the Mahanta had shown me three of my past lives which were all similar. I wish to touch on them here, for they indicate how the Dream Weaver intertwines the working out of personal and world destiny.

The first lifetime shown to me was in China several centuries ago. I had been an official record keeper or librarian for one of the courts. The position allowed me to discover the deceptions that went on behind the official public propaganda. When the rulers started abusing their power over the people, I used my position to write and distribute pamphlets designed to incite the people against their lords. When the rulers discovered my plot, they wasted no time in hunting me down and killing me.

But I must have been a slow learner. In the next past life that I was shown, I had reincarnated into late seventeenth-century Russia. My Jewish upbringing in that life gave me a very good education and taught me how to argue persuasively. Being ideological, I wasted no time in taking up the pen against those in power. The result was, as before, a swift end to that lifetime.

In about 1920, I was born into Berlin, Germany. By the time I was old enough for the university, I had decided to become a writer. Again I was Jewish, and I thought the abuses of the Nazis would make a good subject upon which to vent my "righteous anger." As usual, I was better at writing inflammatory pamphlets than at hiding from my enemies. I was hauled before a local Nazi official, confessed, and was taken out and shot immediately.

45

As I left my body, I was met by an ECK Master. To me it was a tragic moment, but he was chuckling. He said, "You always have to go out the hard way, don't you!" Suddenly my previous lives opened up before me, and I saw the humor in the situation. I resolved then and there that my days of being a political firebrand were over.

I mention these three lifetimes because they were three strands of a karmic cord that the Dream Weaver would help me tie off and finish in 1989. These little personal karmic threads were woven in the great tapestry alongside the convulsions that would rock China, Russia, and Germany in 1989.

* * *

The ECK Springtime Seminar was a great seminar for me. I had a chance to see some old friends and hear the Living ECK Master speak. But what really grabbed my attention was Sri Harold's new book, *Child in the Wilderness*. I couldn't put it down. The book seemed to me a testament of the times, full of prophecies and deep spiritual revelations.

This book describes Sri Harold Klemp's experience of God-Realization, years before he became the Living ECK Master. Of special interest to the theme of this chapter is what happened the night he actually had the God-Realization experience.

In the drama of that night, there is a young woman named Cathy who plays a supporting role, as Harold struggles to reach God while standing on a bridge. When I read that I immediately flashed to my dream experiences with Catherine and the bridge of purification.

And in the climactic scene, as the mighty Light and Sound of God pour into Harold while he is out on the bridge, he experiences a profound purification. Sri Harold writes: "Suddenly I was in the Atma Sarup, at a distance, watching as ages of karma were ripped from me at once. . . . A disease was now gone, but until its absence, I had not even sensed its presence."[6]

After reading that passage, I put the book down. There in Sri Harold's biography was a prototype of my own dream experiences with a Cathy, a bridge, and purification. Of course this doesn't mean everyone will have a literal Cathy-and-the-bridge experience. But in some way expressive of our own nature, each of us will have to experience purification before we can cross our bridge into a new age.

I knew after reading this passage in Sri Harold's book and comparing it to my waking dreams and three past lives mentioned above, that the year would bring great changes into my life. The unresolved karma of those three lives was somehow going to be resolved as part of a world drama that would involve Germany and China. But what could that be?

* * *

By the time I got back home from the San Diego seminar, the Dream Weaver had gathered all the necessary threads for 1989. I saw threads that I think show how the world-shaking events of 1989 parallel the Mahanta's mission:

1. Sri Harold's book *Child in the Wilderness* was a description of taking ECKANKAR and the world across a bridge into a new age, a new consciousness.

2. The initiation and purification Sri Harold had found on the bridge would be reflected in an experience of global initiation and purification.

3. China, Germany, and Russia as key nations in this global transformation.
4. The sacred word of HU would be the catalyst of change throughout the whole process.

The loom was ready, and the weaver was ready to weave!

5

The HU Heard round the World

It all began in honor of a man named Hu. And it began about three weeks after the release of Sri Harold's book *Child in the Wilderness* at the 1989 ECK Springtime Seminar. In *The Universal Almanac 1990,* "The Year in Review," the opening scene is described:

On Apr. 15, 1989, following the death of democratic reformer Hu Yaobang, Chinese students began memorial demonstrations in his honor. These soon swelled into more general, entirely peaceful prodemocracy meetings, marches, and demonstrations in Shanghai, Beijing, and many other cities. By Apr. 18 the demonstrations in Beijing had centered on Tienanmen Square and were swelling in size. On Apr. 20 the government publicly demanded an end to the demonstrations, threatening police action, whereupon Chinese and, to a lesser extent, worldwide media began to pay attention to the developing crisis.[1]

This was the first of many great rallying cries for freedom that would sweep the world in 1989. That the rally began in honor of a man named Hu was for me a striking waking dream of the real cause behind this uprising.

Very swiftly the events in Tienanmen Square moved into the center of world attention. In a rising crescendo throughout the month of May, the cry for change and freedom aroused the global consciousness to hope and inspiration. It is hard to capture in print the euphoria and excitement that swept the world as this drama unfolded.

As the uprising in Tienanmen Square was reaching its point of maximum tension, word came out that ECKANKAR had gained permission to build the Temple of ECK, the first new Golden Wisdom Temple on earth in many thousands of years.

Sri Harold writes,

> May 22, 1989, was an important date in the history of ECKANKAR. On that day, the city council of Chanhassen, Minnesota, approved ECKANKAR's request to build a spiritual edifice.
>
> ECKANKAR has just come through a small window into a new world of being. . . .
>
> Building the Temple followed the laws of creation, whereby the unspoken becomes manifest. Thus the ageless teachings of ECK have found a home in this spiritual age.[2]

In an earlier publication, Sri Harold wrote more on the subject:

> Building the Temple of ECK is an important milestone in the history of ECKANKAR. At its dedication, the ECK Temple will also become the Seat of Power, our spiritual center on earth.
>
> Why a seat of power?
>
> It is a law of the physical world that for a group to survive as long as possible, it must set up a seat of central government. For religions,

this center is the hub for its spiritual activities, administration, and culture.

For now, the Seat of Power for ECKANKAR is in Minnesota. At the crossroads of humanity's quest for spiritual freedom, it is the spiritual center of the world.[3]

I saw the interconnections between the events that were unfolding in China and the building of the Temple of ECK as being subtle but strong. Tienanmen Square is at the heart of Beijing, one of the oldest continuous seats of power in the world. I believe that all great seats of power, whether political or religious, are major etheric centers in the subtle body of earth. They are like chakras, or vortices, through which flow potent spiritual and psychic currents.

When a major new seat of power is established on the planet, it sends reverberations throughout the world. The new vibrations can break up the old established patterns, and instability ensues until a newer and higher harmony can be established. When the new seat of power is a Temple of Golden Wisdom, like the Temple of ECK, the effects can be dramatic.

Paul Twitchell talked about ECKANKAR's need for a seat of power in March 1971 at a leadership training seminar. To illustrate his thesis, Paul discussed some of the famous seats of power around the world. He began: "I jotted down some notes the other night that I thought might be of interest to you because it shows the way that the fulcrum of power works with various nations and various groups. . . . I jotted down seventeen, and I think I'll just read these off."[4]

So often when the Living ECK Master of the time just jots down a few notes or tosses off seemingly casual observations, they are actually the prophetic voice of the ECK speaking through Its vehicle.

Any student of current events should be able to trace the wind of change that blew through some of the seats of power on Paul's list, such as Peking (Beijing), Berlin, and Moscow. So as ECKANKAR's new seat of power got its foothold in physical reality on May 22, humanity's eyes were all on the ancient seat of power in Tienanmen Square in Beijing. As quoted above, the Temple of ECK is "at the crossroads of humanity's quest for spiritual freedom." And Tienanmen Square had become humanity's dramatic stage upon which this spiritual quest was being played out. People all over the world were glued to their television sets, filled with the hope of a new birth of freedom in the world's most populous nation.

A week after the Temple of ECK approval on May 22, the student protesters in Tienanmen Square sculpted a statue they called the white Goddess of Liberty, likened to America's Statue of Liberty.[5] It became their icon of freedom and hope.

By June the tension in China had built to such a point that it was ready to explode. Either there would be a brutal suppression of the demonstrators, or the nation might break into the chaos of a civil war. The third possibility of a peaceful transition to democracy seemed a remote chance but was the one everyone hoped for.

What was happening there inwardly? I believe that as the Temple of ECK was emerging on the world grid of seats of power, the Light and Sound were pouring into China through Tienanmen Square, forcing that nation to make a decision about freedom. The common people in China were responding very positively. But the old Communist regime did not want to relinquish its power. The climactic tension was finally broken on

June 3 when the Chinese rulers ordered tanks into the square against the people, and a bloody massacre ensued which shocked the world.

As I see it, the spiritual force that had built up in Tienanmen Square was so great that a mighty wind of change swept immediately out over the world. Within a twenty-four-hour period of the Beijing massacre, the world's news organizations scrambled to keep up with the sudden burst of headline events from around Eurasia. In its usual way, the world media would fail to see the connections between Tienanmen Square and the other events, but I feel the connections were direct and immediate.

In an article on the Beijing massacre, writer Ray Grasse pointed out these connections based on his study of astrology. In July 1989 he wrote:

> The recent massacre of students in China has already established itself as one of the most dramatic news events in recent times. Almost as extraordinary as the tragedy itself, however, was the uncanny series of historic events that constellated themselves around this same point in time. Within the same 24-hour period, newswatchers had witnessed not only the drama in Tiananmen Square [sic], but the death of Ayatollah Khomeini, a major train disaster in Russia killing hundreds of passengers, ethnic riots in Uzbekistan in the USSR, and the first free elections in modern Polish history.
>
> To the ancients, such clusters of historic events were seen as powerful symbols, suggesting larger transformations in the collective destiny.[6]

Grasse goes on to explain how each of these events could be viewed as turning points in humanity's spiritual unfoldment. For example Ayatollah Khomeini had come to represent an archetype of the fanatical and intolerant religious zealot. He typified the worst traits of the old religious consciousness of a passing age.

For me his death was a waking dream of the blow to such fanaticism coming from the inpouring spiritual currents. This would be seen later that year in the U.S. with the decline of the zealous Moral Majority and the scandals surrounding American evangelists Jim Bakker and Jimmy Swaggart.

Regarding the Polish elections, Grasse displayed keen prophetic insight when he wrote that this revealed "a crack in the communist edifice that could prove to be as far-reaching in its effects for the Soviet Union as the pro-democratic uprisings have been for China."[7] He wrote this in the summer of 1989. By the end of the summer of 1991, the Soviet Union would no longer exist.

Grasse felt the train disaster in Russia was very symbolic. A gas pipeline exploded just as two Soviet trains, going in opposite directions, passed by, killing an estimated five hundred people and injuring hundreds more. He saw this explosion as a metaphor for the imminent clash of opposing political forces that would soon derail the entire Soviet Union, breaking the world's largest empire to pieces.

The dam that had burst in China on June 3 temporarily eased the buildup of tension in the network of world seats of power. While the authors I have quoted have their own interpretation of the causes of these events, I feel that the negative forces were struggling to block the liberating energies that were pouring into the world because of the emerging Temple of ECK. The attack on the demonstrators in Tienanmen Square was a futile attempt by these negative forces to hold back the flow. But the rising tide of Light and

Sound simply swept outward from China in a wide circle that washed over the Asian continent.

*   *   *

On a more personal note, there were events in my own life that were influenced by events surrounding the building of the Temple of ECK. At 8:30 a.m., September 11, 1989, I walked into the front office of a large retail company in Oregon. It was my first day of work in a new profession. Two years earlier I had quit a high-paying profession in the aerospace industry to take a gamble on a new career. The choice had been an agonizing one. After months of indecision, I had turned it over to the Inner Master. The night I did this, Sri Harold showed me in a dream that it was the correct move to make. Little did I know that by 1991 the Cold War would be declared over, devastating the aerospace job market I had left behind.

At the moment I was walking through that door to start a new life, it was 10:30 a.m. in Chanhassen, Minnesota. There Sri Harold was pushing a shovel into the prairie sod for the ground-breaking ceremony for the Temple of ECK. I wouldn't learn of the ground-breaking ceremony until several weeks later. This was the second key date in the history of the Temple of ECK which coincided precisely with a big day in my life. The first had been the permission to build the Temple of ECK on May 22, my wedding anniversary.

September 11, 1989, stands as one of the most important dates in the spiritual journey of the human race. The visible effects of the Temple ground breaking on the world were immediate and far-reaching. The mass uprising in China described earlier had begun in honor of a man named Hu. This same word *HU*, which is an ancient name for God, would be involved

55

symbolically in two other events which happened on September 11.

The first event unfolded in the nation of Hungary. Hungary, by the way, is the only nation in the world that begins with *H-u!* The seeds of what happened in Hungary were quietly planted in May, when everyone was watching the mass uprising in Tienanmen Square. Hungary had started removing the barbed-wire fence that had stretched between it and Austria since 1949.[8]

This action didn't go unnoticed by the East Germans, many of whom were eager to circumvent the closed border between East Germany and West. From May through August, a trickle, and then a river, of intrepid East Germans were slipping into the West over the Hungarian-Austrian border. The East German rulers were irate and began to protest to the Hungarians.

By early September, thousands of East Germans were crowding into Hungary in hopes of escaping to the West. Late on the night of September 11, the same day Sri Harold held the ground-breaking ceremony for the Temple of ECK in Minnesota, the Hungarian government suddenly threw open its borders and allowed over ten thousand East Germans to escape.

As reporters for *Time* magazine wrote, "That night, shortly after midnight, Hungary began permitting East German refugees to cross over en masse into Austria. [East Germans watching West German television] realized that the Iron Curtain had parted."[9]

By September 12, there was a virtual stampede of people fleeing to the West through the hole in the Iron Curtain. For all practical purposes, the Iron Curtain became history on that day. The flood of East Germans pouring through Hungary would lead within eight weeks to the fall of the Berlin Wall.

This rush of freedom rapidly swept out into humanity. The same liberation euphoria that had burst forth in Tienanmen Square in May had just resurfaced on the opposite side of Eurasia.

What was happening here? My own feeling is that the initial wave of Divine Spirit that sparked the mass urge to freedom in China in honor of a man named Hu began with the permission to build the Temple of ECK. On June 3 that divine wave had seemingly been smothered by the negative forces in a brutal massacre in Tienanmen Square.

But the wave had simply moved westward. The second mass urge to freedom occurred in Hungary and coincided with the Temple ground-breaking ceremony. The momentum was building, and the negative forces could no longer even pretend to hold back the cry for liberation. The Wind of Change was blowing. It seemed to be moving westward. Where would it go next? On September 12 a tropical storm began to form off the coast of West Africa. The weather officials named it Hugo. Once again, notice the word *HU* in Hugo!

The name *Hugo* comes from *Hugh* in the old German language. The meaning of the name *Hugo* is very telling. One translation is "heart" or "mind."[10] Another is "Soul."[11] Yet another rendition is "servant of the spirit."[12]

If I put all these translations together, I come up with: "Hugo, a servant of Spirit in heart, mind, and Soul." But how could a hurricane be an agent of liberation and a servant of Spirit? How would Hugo carry forward the wave of liberation? To me, writers Bob and Celeste Longacre reveal the key in a very perceptive article on Hurricane Hugo.

They write that Hurricane Hugo "formed off of Western Africa, moved west over the sunken continent of Atlantis, passed over the islands of Guadeloupe, Montserrat, the U.S. Virgin Islands, and Puerto Rico and finally focused on Charleston, South Carolina. All of these places had been involved in slavery. . . ."

Further, they note that "South Carolina was the first state to secede from the Union (Dec. 20, 1860) and Fort Sumter in Charleston Harbor (heavily damaged by Hugo) was where the first shots of the Civil War were fired."[13]

In other words, I see that the liberating wave of HU, as it swept across the Atlantic from the Old World to the New, was continuing its theme of liberation by cleaning out a centuries-old karmic trail of slavery. This trail of slavery and subjugation was perhaps the worst historic connection between the two hemispheres.

On the inner planes, I saw this storm begin to expose the poor state of race relations in the United States. The issue of racism and inequality would come very strongly before the public after years of being ignored. And one of the worst race riots in American history would shake Los Angeles and other cities in 1992. Even the nation which most embodied racial division—South Africa—would soon take an unexpected turn toward the resolution of apartheid, or racial segregation.

But the wave of HU was not yet finished. It rolled on across the United States. Then, on October 17, 1989, as the earthmovers were digging to lay the Temple's foundation, an earthquake shook the West Coast, bringing heavy damage to San Francisco. Within twenty-four hours, the architect of the Berlin Wall, Erich Honecker, resigned as leader of East Germany.[14]

All this dramatic world change, and only the foundation had been laid at the Temple of ECK! On November 9, 1989, workers began the vertical structure of the Temple of ECK.[15] That this first skyward gesture occurred on the ninth day of the month is significant. I feel it was symbolic of humanity's dream of reaching toward the Ninth Plane of God.

The very day these walls started to go up, the greatest liberation euphoria of the year, perhaps of the century, swept the world as the Berlin Wall was opened. On November 9, people climbed up and danced on the Wall. The Cold War was effectively over, and the walls came tumbling down. This day was one of the climactic moments of the twentieth century.

Here is a remarkable story that could easily become a legend. A Higher Initiate in ECK was in Berlin the weekend that the Wall came down. He was on his way from West Berlin to East Berlin to give a talk on ECKANKAR. Because of the disruption caused by the decision to open the wall, the processing of the H.I.'s papers was taking several hours. As he sat in his car waiting, a woman who had just come through from the East ran up to him excitedly. She just wanted to share her excitement and the wonder of her sudden freedom.

She showed the ECKist the stamp in her passport, which was the same two-letter code being stamped in all the passports of those going West for the first time that day. It was simply a two-letter code—HU.

The day the Berlin Wall opened was one of the happiest days of my life. The Mahanta had shown me earlier in the week that the world was going to get a sort of initiation. On November 5 I had written in my dream diary, "Something the Mahanta referred to as 'Freedom Weekend' is coming this weekend. Expect important news." I knew that no matter what reversals might happen in coming months and years, the human race had taken a giant spiritual step forward. I wrote in my dream journal that weekend in giant letters, "FREEDOM WEEKEND," and under the heading recorded the following dream:

> I float out of the body, and head in a beeline straight for Berlin, where thousands of people are celebrating on the Berlin Wall. To my happy surprise I spot a group of about fifteen ECK Masters nearby. They are laughing and slapping each other on the back. One of the Masters says, "We've worked a very long, very hard time to bring this about."

I didn't recognize any of these ECK Masters as ones known to the world or in the writings of ECKANKAR. Their mission was to help the Mahanta by working quietly behind the scenes with the nations of Europe.

As so often happens at historically critical moments, a series of waking dreams appear. As the walls of the Temple of ECK went up and the Berlin Wall came down, a number of other "wall" images were circulating in the public consciousness. Writer Marcia Montenegro noticed these:

1. The Reverend Ralph David Abernathy stirred up debates with a new controversial biography on Martin Luther King, Jr., titled *And the Walls Came Tumbling Down.* This tied in with Hurricane Hugo's cleansing of the Atlantic slave routes, as Martin Luther King was the nation's modern visionary of racial justice and harmony. The book's title was an uncanny parallel to the fall of the Berlin Wall.

2. Wall Street suffered a dramatic 190-point downslide a few days before the San Francisco quake.

3. Hurricane Hugo had demolished many of the seawalls of the South Carolina coast.[16]

Again, while Montenegro viewed these events through the lens of astrology, I could see that all of these sweeping outer changes were just reflections of inner changes. The world was going through a profound spiritual transformation. In early 1989 I had a heart-touching inner experience which hinted at this and showed me how ECKists are vehicles for the Mahanta's mission.

In a dream, I found myself in Europe, sitting with a large crowd of people on the free side of the Iron Curtain. Across a sort of barren no-man's-land, another crowd sat opposite us. There was a leader speaking to each of the crowds. The leader on my side was saying, "You must have patience! You can't trust the Communists. Change must come very slowly, one step at a time." I felt bored by this self-appointed leader, and I could sense most of the crowd was just as impatient as I was.

Suddenly, I just stood up and started walking out into the no-man's-land toward the other side. The leader shouted hysterically, "You fool! You'll get killed!" As I walked, I saw that a woman from the other side had gotten up and was walking toward me. We met in the middle and shook hands. She asked, "Are you an ECKist?" I smiled and said, "Yes! Are you?" She said yes and told me her name. Though I had never met her physically, I knew her to be a respected Higher Initiate in Europe. We laughed together.

At that moment, crowds from both sides got to their feet and, ignoring their leaders, simply walked to the middle and started mingling very naturally.

More than anything else, the year 1989 was a year of perfect timing for me. Dates became important. I realize there are many who view time as an illusion unworthy of serious consideration. But no one becomes an ECK Master without mastering the Law of Economy. And this law governs the proper use of time and energy in the lower worlds.

Fortunately, it isn't necessary to put a lot of attention on cycles and dates to work with this law. One needs simply to learn to follow the inner guidance of the Mahanta. But whether one wishes to become aware of it or not, there is a vast master plan through which the Mahanta unfolds his mission. This plan must be brought forth in the right order and at the right time to be fully effective. One purpose of this book is to make clear the existence of such a master plan.

In 1989 I received an inner initiation on my father's birthday. The pink slip for the outer initiation arrived in the mail on my mother's birthday a few months later. I would later come to realize how my initiation, and many thousands of other people's as well, was linked directly to the Temple of ECK. To the initiate, the initiation seems a very personal affair. But I believe that in the vast scheme of things, it is a part of a wider planetary unfoldment in which multitudes of Souls are participating.

A book could be written on how all these individual initiations are woven together by the Mahanta into a vast spiritual plan. Together we become the universal body of the Mahanta. It is far greater than the sum of its parts. This subject will be explored in the last chapter of this book.

The following short list is a quick review of just a few of the ways the HU, and the building of the Temple of ECK, was felt around the world in 1989.

- May 22, 1989: ECKANKAR gains permission from the Chanhassen City Council to build the Temple of ECK. A massive popular uprising in honor of a man named Hu nears its climax in China.

- September 11, 1989: Sri Harold Klemp breaks ground for the Temple. The Communist nation of Hungary opens its borders to the West, effectively opening the Iron Curtain.
- September 12, 1989: Hurricane Hugo cleans out racial karma along the old Atlantic slave-trade routes.
- October 17, 1989: As construction workers move ground for the foundation of the Temple, an earthquake shakes San Francisco. It happens just before a televised World Series baseball game and so is witnessed by millions of people, as far away as Japan. The next day, the architect of the Berlin Wall and leader of East Germany steps down from power.
- November 9, 1989: As the construction workers begin to erect the walls of the Temple, the Berlin Wall is opened, ending forty years of division in Europe. Citizens from East Germany passing through the Wall to enjoy a weekend of freedom in West Berlin have *H-U* stamped in their passports.

In a fitting tribute to all this, on October 22, 1989, Sri Harold proclaimed the spiritual year the Year of the HU.

* * *

Having swept clear around the world, inwardly and outwardly, where was there left for HU to go? All one had to do was look at the Temple of ECK. In April 1990 construction workers began putting the crown on the Temple—the ziggurat roof.

I feel this nine-stepped pyramid symbolizes

humanity's dream of reaching far beyond the earth world, into the pure worlds of God. I saw this reflected in a waking dream. In April 1990, the American space shuttle *Discovery* launched into orbit the world's first optical space telescope, named the Edwin P. Hubble Space Telescope. (Please note the letters *H-u* in Hubble!)

To me, this instrument symbolized a number of things. It symbolized the sacred word HU, springing from the hearts and lips of the human race, soaring into space. It symbolized the world's search for the Star of ECK, which is the Blue Star of the Mahanta.

One of the main missions of the Hubble telescope is to search for evidence of planets in other solar systems, symbolizing a search for community. The *HU* in *Hubble* represents for me a call from planet Earth to the universe, a longing to join a greater community.

Shortly after being launched, space scientists discovered the Hubble had a faulty mirror and wasn't seeing as perfectly as had been hoped. Which, of course, is an apt statement for what was happening down on earth. We, the human race, tasted the joy and spiritual release of HU in 1989. But we have much to learn. Our spiritual vision is not yet clear. Our dreams still outrun our ability to express them. The world is yet marred with strife, selfishness, and tribal feuding.

Hence, I feel that the ziggurat represents not attainment but a goal of humanity. The Mahanta has put the Temple of ECK here on earth as a promise of what we can all attain. Whether we rise to our potential is as yet uncertain. This will be explored in the chapter on global initiation.

I saw one more incident connected with the Temple of ECK. It came shortly after the Temple Dedication in October, 1990. The yearning of the human race to see more clearly and deeply was expressed in the world's most powerful reflector telescope, the W.M. Keck Telescope.[17] Note the word *ECK* in Keck.

The words *Hubble* and *Keck* contain the two sacred words HU (an ancient name for God; also a sacred prayer song) and ECK (the Light and Sound of God, Divine Spirit). The telescopes are both optical, or light-sensing, telescopes. Hence, they signify for me the world's new yearning for the Light and Sound of God. It is the mission and the destiny of the Temple of ECK to give this Light and Sound to the whole world.

This chapter has traced what I see as the effects of the Temple of ECK in the world during 1989 and 1990. I focused mainly on the changes that occurred in the sphere of political freedom, because they were so obvious and dramatic. But equally great changes were being effected in all departments of life on our planet. And all of these changes were but the outer effects of the most important change of all: the spiritual one. I see these changes as the by-product of the Mahanta's main goal, to bring the gospel of spiritual liberation to the world.

6

Reverberations from the Past

Sri Harold has brought us a lot of spiritual gold.
At various times he has spoken about the Golden
Heart; the Golden Age of ECK; the Golden-tongued
Wisdom; and our own Golden Wisdom Temple, the
Temple of ECK, with its golden ziggurat roof, its gold-
toned walls, and golden trim. And in fact, if you draw
a rectangle over the outline of the Temple of ECK, the
ratio of the length of the long and short sides is very
close to the golden, or divine, proportion.

One morning on the way to work, I jotted down the
list of spiritual gold in the above paragraph. When I
got to work, I found a message on my telephone an-
swering machine. It was from a co-worker. Her message was brief and absolutely perfect: "Jim, it's me. I
checked out the project, and it's as good as gold."

Much of this spiritual gold had once been available
to the world in times past, but it had been lost. The
recovery of this lost spiritual wealth was now mani-
festing with the Temple of ECK. The Temple's birth
brought forth a great wave of spiritual freedom in the
world. And with this great spiritual treasure also came
storms of unresolved karma.

So often we view unresolved karma as a curse from the past. But in its resolution comes a release from age-old burdens, allowing us to step forward.

Likewise if we have any hidden weaknesses, there is nothing like a spiritual step forward to bring them swiftly to the surface for all to see. How often have we boasted that we are above anger, greed, or vanity, only to find ourselves once again caught in their web?

The same process works on world levels. Just as Eastern Europe rejoiced in its new freedom after the collapse of the Iron Curtain, it suddenly found itself mired in ethnic rivalries from the past. The ECK brings people the gift of greater freedom, but the price is the letting go of old passions and attachments. This theme will be discussed in more depth in the chapter on global initiation. But it pertains to this chapter also.

Two stories emerged in the world media at the time of the Temple ground-breaking ceremony which were about lost treasure that was found. Both stories appeared to me to be waking dreams about reverberations from the past set in motion by the birth of the new Temple. As Sri Harold was bringing spiritual gold back into the world, actual physical treasures of gold were also found. And as we shall see, these physical treasures have an interesting story to tell.

The first story begins in 1848, during the California gold rush.[1] In those days, to avoid the long and dangerous overland route to the West, many people would sail south to the Isthmus of Panama, cross over by train, and then catch a ship up the West Coast to California. When going back, they would retrace the same route. One of the ships which sailed the Atlantic leg of the journey was the 272-foot *Central America,* a wooden vessel.

She set sail for New York from Panama in September 1857, laden with three tons of gold and 578 people. On Thursday, September 10, the *Central America* was hit by the fierce winds of an approaching hurricane. By the next day, the hurricane was upon her, and the vessel was taking on water. Saturday, September 12, at 8:00 p.m., she went down, with all her gold and most of the passengers.

This incident, which occurred on September 10, 11, and 12 of 1857, happened exactly 132 years before the Temple ground breaking, which was on September 11, 1989.

The author of the article wrote, "For months, the sinking was front-page news. Then, as the Civil War neared, the *Central America* was pushed from the public's mind. In time, all memory of it vanished— except in the lore of treasure seekers and historians."[2]

The sinking of the *Central America* in 1857 as the United States moved toward civil war was a national waking dream. I saw the message as being "The winds of change will soon blow across America, plunging the treasure of the Union into a deep abyss." The connection of this waking dream to the Temple is revealed in the second half of the story.

In the twentieth century, a man named Tommy Thompson became obsessed with the story of the *Central America*. He set his mind to discover the lost treasure at any cost. By the end of 1986, the year ECKANKAR moved its office to Minneapolis, Thompson completed an underwater recovery vehicle. He named it Nemo after the captain in *Twenty Thousand Leagues Under the Sea*. Throughout 1987, 1988, and early 1989, as the Mahanta made steady progress toward establishing the Temple of ECK, Thompson and his crew made steady progress in their search for the sunken treasure. Each exploration brought more bits and pieces of the sunken ship. Finally, in early September of 1989, roughly when Sri Harold was performing his ground-breaking ceremony for the new Temple, the crew was recovering, after many delays, about one ton of gold.

But a very curious replay of history occurred shortly after this recovery operation began. Hurricane Hugo began off the coast of Africa in September 1989. Just as the hurricane of September 1857 had borne down on the *Central America,* now Hurricane Hugo bore down on Thompson's recovery ship. The storm drove him and his crew back to the coast of North Carolina.

As I mentioned in the chapter "The HU Felt round the World," Hurricane Hugo struck locations that had been involved with the slave trade. It was the slave trade and its consequences which sowed the seeds of the American Civil War. Hurricane Hugo was a mighty wind that cleansed much of that ancient karma.

Yet another golden thread in this story concerns the state of Minnesota, where the new Temple was built. Minnesota took its first step toward statehood in 1857 when it drew up its state constitution. It would enter the Union the following year on May 11 as the thirty-second state. Hence the *Central America* sunk the same year Minnesota was being born.

The detail and accuracy of these ancient and modern waking dreams are very striking. I believe that even the 132-year span that separates the past and present events is a cycle tied to the Temple of ECK. For 132 years is a multiple of eleven. If this were a book on the sacred numbers of the ECK-Vidya, a chapter could easily be written on the number eleven and the Temple of ECK. In my notes I have accumulated many pages on this subject. A very few examples are:

1. Minnesota entered the Union on May 11.
2. The permission to build the Temple of ECK came on May 22. (22=11 x 2).
3. The Temple ground breaking occurred on September 11.
4. The Temple Dedication occurred on October 22.

Why do I think the Temple of ECK is so attuned to this number? The key is given in Paul Twitchell's book *The ECK-Vidya: Ancient Science of Prophecy*. Paul writes: "Number 11 is the number of instruction, either in the position of being instructed in the arts of the ancient wisdoms, or being the Master who gives the instructions."[3] And this is the purpose of the Temples of Golden Wisdom: To instruct us in the ancient wisdoms of the ECK.

* * *

The second story of lost treasure found comes out of the mists of ancient history. The week after the ECK Worldwide Seminar in October 1989, *Time* magazine published a story titled "The Golden Treasures of Nimrud."[4] Nimrud was a glorious fortress city, located in modern-day Iraq. It was first built in about 1250 B.C. and rebuilt during the height of the Assyrian Empire from around 900 B.C. to 612 B.C.

The centerpiece of the city was a ziggurat-towered palace. In the rubble of the now-crumbled ziggurat, archaeologists discovered a tomb filled with 125.6 pounds of gold jewelry. *Time* correspondent Philip Elmer-De Witt writes, "John Curtis, an archaeologist from the British Museum, describes the treasure of Nimrud as the most significant archaeological discovery since King Tutankhamen's tomb was uncovered in Egypt in 1922."

How does this discovery tie in to the Temple of

71

ECK? In a number of important ways. More than a waking dream, I feel this discovery unleashed on the world ancient and unresolved karma in the form of the Gulf War of 1991. But before we explore that karmic time bomb, let us tie in a few loose threads.

In the fall of 1989, Sri Harold wrote of the new Temple of ECK:

> A pale golden ziggurat crowns the temple. The stepped, pyramidal roof is reminiscent of architecture common to ancient Sumer, Babylonia, and Assyria. The design symbolizes mankind's spiritual journey up the plateaus of life.[5]

In the Winter of 1989 Sri Harold picked up this theme again when discussing the Temple as a seat of power for ECKANKAR:

> Five to six thousand years ago, the ancient Sumerians built temples for their gods and goddesses in every village. Sumer was where Iraq is today. Villagers believed that the deities who lived in these temples protected them. By 2000 B.C. the capital city of Ur had constructed a temple called a ziggurat. It was a tower made of mud bricks, which narrowed at the top like a pyramid. The roof of the ECK Temple is reminiscent of the ancient design.[6]

Sri Harold goes on to explain why he was reviewing this period in history. It was because many ECK chelas of today lived in those ancient times, farmed the soil in what is modern-day Iraq, and worshiped at the ziggurat temples.

In other words, people have come again today to continue their spiritual unfoldment. The Sumerian civilization was the wellspring of the Middle-Eastern religions which spread over the world. Even Judaism, elder brother to Christianity and Islam, can trace many of its religious legends and myths to ancient Sumeria.

The Temple of ECK reopened the door to that ancient time and carried forward into the modern world the accumulated treasure of thousands of years of spiritual growth. Hence the symbol of the treasure of gold found in an ancient ziggurat in Iraq and the Temple ground breaking within months of each other.

But the opening of that door to the past also meant unlocking an ancient, sinister karma. The Lords of Karma are patient. The wheel of cause and effect may turn slowly, but it inevitably comes around again. In hindsight, one can see in this Iraqi treasure story a prophecy of the coming Gulf War. How?

The *Time* article says the ancient city of Nimrud "was once the military capital of one of history's fiercest empires."[7] I feel their brutality marked the final stage—a dark age, a Kali Yuga—of that period in history.

Says *Time* writer Elmer-De Witt: "They were known for their ferocious cruelty. In addition to their biblical role as the oppressors of Israel, there was the testimony of Ashurnasirpal II, an Assyrian king of the 9th century B.C. who boasted in cuneiform inscriptions of having rebellious chieftains impaled on stakes" and tortured to death.[8]

Iraqi dictator Saddam Hussein professed to dream of reestablishing the power of such ancient kings. He was notorious for the torture and execution of any subordinates who resisted his will. This reflected Ashurnasirpal's penchant for handling rebellious chieftains. Hussein's invasion of Kuwait on August 2, 1990, surprised the world and quickly sent shock waves of concern and fear through the world community. The Scud missiles he sent raining on Israel were reminiscent of the ancient Assyrians' oppression of that land.

The tentacles of this ancient karma spread rapidly over the earth, entangling practically all the nations of the world to one extent or another.

When Sri Harold wrote that many modern-day ECKists had ties to ancient Sumeria/Assyria, I knew very well that I was one. My unresolved karmic involvement was a mixture of both worthy and ignoble past lives. The Mahanta helped me resolve a great deal of karma during the time of the Gulf Crisis. But he also blessed me with many wonderful insights on the Temple of ECK. It was a bittersweet experience.

It began the day Iraqi forces invaded Kuwait on August 2. In the late months of 1990, I found myself on the inner planes in a distasteful position. I, along with a number of other people, was assigned to visit Iraqi diplomats and try to find a peaceful solution. One episode was a lesson in humility.

I had to sit patiently with a group of about fifteen other Americans and listen to Iraqi military leaders tell their side of the story. They were very convincing about how the Kuwaitis had wronged their nation and were stealing their country's oil by drilling slanted shafts beneath the border.

The real work of karmic cleansing for me came unexpectedly on the day the so-called "ground war" began. Within an hour after the allies counterattacked on the ground against the Iraqis, I came down with excruciatingly painful sinusitis. For days I could do nothing to escape the pain. I lay in bed suffering miserably.

During this time, I would frequently slip out of the body. The Mahanta would assign me immediately to go into the trenches to do what I could to ease the pain of wounded and dying Iraqi soldiers.

On one occasion I saw a number of Higher Initiates

in ECK doing the same work. It was a difficult and emotionally fatiguing effort. But these Brothers of the Leaf gave no thought as to which side the wounded and dying were on. Loving assistance was provided wherever it would help.

About one hundred hours after the ground war began, President Bush announced Iraq had surrendered. The Iraqi resistance had been overestimated, and the allied counter-invasion suffered relatively few casualties. The Iraqi soldiers and people themselves had not been so fortunate.

Within an hour or so of the surrender, my sinusitis symptoms disappeared. A major karmic cleansing from ages ago had just been effected in the world. There were many lessons in this for me. A big one was the realization of how often the good and bad karma of past lives is intertwined. One often gets both coming back at the same time.

This was true for humanity at large. The Temple of ECK had brought forth a great wave of spiritual freedom in the world. With it came the treasure of good karma from ancient times and a dose of bad karma from the same ancient times. Yet after all, it was humanity itself that had earned the mixed blessings symbolized in the discovery of both the gold and the curse in a crumbled Iraqi ziggurat.

*   *   *

The two stories told above show vividly how we can perceive waking dreams on national and world levels with the same facility as we do in our individual lives.

I have been asked a number of times how I discover the type of connections described above. The technique is really quite simple. When I write down personal experiences in my journal, I also write down what is happening in my community or in the world at the same time. This is especially important if I feel moved by what is happening in the news at that time. Periodically I'll go back through my journal and look for the golden thread that ties the individual narratives together.

Each of us is a microcosm of the macrocosm. We are a cell in the body of humanity. What affects the whole, affects the part, and vice versa. Once we recognize this, we begin to realize how the Mahanta works with all of us. For each time one of us takes a step forward spiritually, the whole world is lifted a little.

7

Field of Dreams

Filmmakers can be wonderfully responsive to ideas flowing from the Mahanta, even if they may not always recognize it when their films are inspired by the ECK. But movies are one of the most effective ways of putting forth visions into the mind of the public.

The ECK Masters depend on the Law of Economy to get the most return for the least effort. And they surely realize the exceptional opportunities of working inwardly with receptive artists. A single inspired film can transform the minds and hearts of millions of viewers.

Certain years are almost defined or summed up by one outstanding movie. In 1989, the year construction began on the Temple of ECK, *Field of Dreams* was such a film for me. It captured the hearts of moviegoers all over America with its subtle blending of dreams and imagination, baseball and farming. Among many ECKists it was an instant hit and moved to the top of their best-movie-ever list.

But *Field of Dreams* was much more than a delightful and heartwarming movie. It was a wondrous expression of the themes of the Temple of ECK. May 22, 1989, was the day ECKANKAR received permission from the Chanhassen City Council to build the Temple. Sri Harold's first public appearance after this event came a few weeks later at the 1989 ECK Creative Arts Festival in Orlando, Florida. At that seminar he gave a talk titled "Field of Dreams" about the movie and another titled "The Temple of ECK." In his characteristic way, Sri Harold made only subtle connections between the movie and the Temple of ECK in that talk. But he was putting the attention of the ECKists on it.

To show how the movie ties in with the Temple of ECK, I'll give a brief review of the plot. A sixties radical named Ray Kinsella (played by Kevin Costner) has married and settled down to farm corn in Iowa. He doesn't know a lot about farming and is having to struggle to make it. One day while out in his cornfield, he has a mystical experience. He hears a voice whisper, "If you build it, he will come."

Ray understands that if he plows under a section of his cornfield and builds a baseball diamond, then "he" will come. To the ridicule and laughter of his neighbors, he follows the instruction and builds the baseball field.

Then the voice tells Ray to "ease his pain." And he discovers he must go find a once-famous sixties writer who has become a recluse and try to ease his loneliness and pain by getting him to go to a baseball game. Baseball was once the great love of the lonely writer, and it is just what he needs to break out of his pain.

Ray must go against common sense, face ingratitude, and surmount all sorts of obstacles to follow the instructions. But in doing so, he is finally able to ease the pain of the writer. Then the subplots of the writer and the baseball field start to come together. The baseball field becomes a magical doorway between the outer world of an Iowa farm and the inner world of dreams and imagination. An old baseball team from the early 1900s, who had been expelled permanently from professional baseball over a scandal, comes through the doorway from beyond death to finally finish their unfulfilled dreams. Eventually, even Ray's father, with whom he had a very difficult relationship, comes back from the other worlds to heal their emotional wounds.

An interesting quality of *Field of Dreams* is that, at first, only those who believe in the baseball field can see the players. Later, as the consciousness of the people begins to raise, more and more people can see the field. They are strongly attracted to it, because they sense it is a place to fulfill their dreams.

By the end of the story, thousands of people from all over are spontaneously drawn to the magical field, and it becomes a place of pilgrimage.

Now it will be clearer to see the association of the movie to the Temple of ECK. Like the field of dreams, the Temple of ECK was built in a field in the heartland of America. Like the field, it too is a doorway between the inner and outer worlds, a place where people can come to fulfill their dreams.

At first, only those who strongly believed in the field of dreams could see the players who were there. Later, as more believed and had the experience, more could see. So it is with the Temple of ECK. The Mahanta and the Vairagi ECK Masters of the Temple of ECK are invisible to all but the faithful at first. But as time passes, more and more people around the world will begin to recognize their existence and see them inwardly.

And now that the Temple of ECK is built, it will gradually become a magnet that draws people from all over to come to it.

The voice that guided Ray Kinsella to build a

baseball diamond in his cornfield is the voice of divine guidance. To me it is the ECK, the Mahanta. I see this movie as both a description of the process of building the Temple of ECK and a prophecy of its future.

I went to see the movie *Field of Dreams* in the summer of 1989. As I walked out of the theater after the show, I had an intuitive feeling that this movie held some deep secrets on the Mahanta's mission. And that night I had a dream with Sri Harold which would confirm this for me.

In the dream, I was standing in the field in Chanhassen where the ECK Temple was soon to be built. Sri Harold walked up to me and shook hands. Then he said, "Did you know there used to be a baseball diamond here many years ago? Come on, let's see if we can find the bases!"

We walked out over the field, looking for any remnants of the diamond. Suddenly Sri Harold said, "Look! Here's where home base was!" Sure enough, there was just a little remnant of a wooden stake marking home base. "Now, if we walk in that direction we should find first base," he explained. I followed him as he counted his paces. Soon he stopped and said, "Here is where first base was, but there's nothing left anymore." Then we headed off to find second base.

After counting his paces again, Sri Harold came to the spot where he thought second base should be. "Dig here," he said. I took a stick and dug out a little bit of dirt, then hit something hard. "That's it!" he exclaimed. I was very excited too. Digging down as fast as I could, I uncovered the top few inches of an old iron rod. Sri Harold looked at me thoughtfully and said, "This will be the exact entrance to the Temple of ECK."

Then, referring to earlier years when he was second baseman on the ECKANKAR team back in California,

80

Sri Harold said, "Of course, it wasn't a coincidence that I was a second baseman."

When I awoke from this dream, I was puzzled about the significance of second base as the exact entrance to the soon-to-be-built Temple. I would have to wait more than two years before the full meaning of the dream was given to me. But there was enough of an understanding to start working with the elements of the dream.

Nineteen eighty-nine was very much a year of baseball. First, there was the movie *Field of Dreams.* Second, one of the game's greatest players, Pete Rose, was in the news all year about his gambling problems and, like the players in *Field of Dreams,* was excluded from the game. Third, the World Series in San Francisco was interrupted by a strong earthquake. This happened before a broadcast audience of millions of people. And as mentioned previously, the earthquake coincided within twenty-four hours with the resignation of East Germany's dictator Erich Honecker, the architect of the Berlin Wall. This showed me how world events are subtly connected to each other and to the Temple of ECK.

Why was 1989 the year of baseball? To me it has much to do with the Temple of ECK and the Mahanta's mission. But the connection may not be obvious. Baseball is more than a sport in America, more than a pastime. It is part of our national character, an expression of some part of the American psyche that creates a unique fascination.

There are some elements of the sport that help create this aura. Many games are metaphors for some part of life: the tests, the challenges, the journey, the community, and the competition. But perhaps baseball is unique in expressing symbolically the spiritual process involved in building the Temple of ECK. What is that? The process of bringing together the currents of ECK from the worlds of God and a structure in the physical world.

For example, the spiritual currents of ECK are keyed to the number nine, as is the game of baseball. In *The ECK-Vidya: Ancient Science of Prophecy* Paul Twitchell writes, "The law of numbers does not belong to the realm of chance. Numbers are potent factors in the working out of divine law."[1] About the number nine, Paul writes, "The number 9 which is sometimes called the ninth path of the ECK is the pure essence of the spirit current which flows out of the SUGMAD and which is called the ECK, or the audible life stream."[2]

The whole structure of the game of baseball is built on the number nine. There are nine players on each team. The game is played in nine periods called innings. There are ninety feet between each of the four bases. The ball itself is nine inches in circumference. The heart of the playing field is a little circular mound of dirt called the pitcher's mound, which has a nine-foot radius. So the number nine is the first part of the baseball metaphor and represents the action of the ECK, or Divine Spirit.

The second part of the metaphor is the diamond-shaped playing field. In *The ECK-Vidya: Ancient Science of Prophecy* Paul writes, "The diamond . . . is related to the physical world and man's human experience. It represents *divine power brought to bear upon the material conditions*" [italics mine].[3]

If you put the two parts together, you see baseball as a wonderfully rich metaphor for the process of building the Temple of ECK. And I submit that this is more than a metaphor. It is a mandala, a blueprint for a spiritual process.

I believe that the theme of Sri Harold's mission and the Temple of ECK is to bring together Divine Spirit (the number nine) and the physical world (the diamond). A remarkably prophetic expression of this baseball theme is in Sri Harold's biography, *Soul Travelers of the Far Country*. There he finds some of the last big tests he faces before becoming the Living ECK Master are played out on a baseball diamond while he is part of the ECKANKAR baseball team.

Just as Sri Harold's experience of God-Realization on the bridge in Wisconsin foretold his mission of leading ECKANKAR across a bridge into a new age, his final trials of training for Mastership in 1981 on a baseball diamond foretold his mission of building the Temple of ECK. It would be a struggle, but a victorious one.

Other "coincidences" of baseball and the Temple of ECK concern the Minnesota Twins baseball team. Against incredible odds, the team won the World Series in 1987, the year following ECKANKAR's move to Minneapolis, Minnesota.

And they did it again, against the odds, winning the World Series in 1991. That second championship took place side by side with the first ECK Worldwide Seminar in Minneapolis, as thousands of ECKists converged in Minnesota to see the Temple of ECK for the first time.

Everywhere in the city were the words "Win Twins." This was the amazing climax of the intertwining of baseball and the Temple of ECK. It was a masterpiece of the Dream Weaver's art.

While writing this chapter, I became curious whether the Minnesota team's luck was tied to the Mahanta's work in the past. Sure enough, the first time Minnesota won a major-league pennant was in

1965, the year Paul Twitchell founded modern-day ECKANKAR. A curious parallel indeed.

This isn't meant to imply that God favors the Twins over any other team. It is just a law of Divine Spirit that the outer worlds reflect the inner ones, and baseball appears to be an outer metaphor for one part of the Mahanta's mission. We shall see in the chapter "The Universal Body of the Mahanta" how the Temple of ECK is related to the form of a baseball diamond.

Later in this book I discuss some of the cosmic cycles to which the Temple of ECK is keyed. Many of the cycles, numbers, and dimensions associated with the Temple of ECK can be found in the dimensions of the baseball field. The whole baseball playing field is an inspired diagram of these numbers.

The point of this chapter is not to mystify the sport of baseball but only to demonstrate how the Mahanta's mission shows up in the most unexpected places. Who would expect a mere game to serve the purposes of the spiritual hierarchy?

Too often people are apt to think the hand of God is to be seen mainly in the field of religion. It is equally at work in all human activities. And the ECK may even touch more people through the medium of sports, for example, than through overt religion.

A sports fan who is indifferent to religion may have a fascination for baseball. Though he will likely be unconscious of what is happening, his focused interest on that sport can instill in him subtle spiritual lessons. The genius of the movie *Field of Dreams* is just this: it appeals equally to both the spiritual and the secular consciousness. Millions of viewers who may never hear of the Temple of ECK were uplifted and came away with a broader vision of life after seeing this film.

8

For All Mankind

The Dedication to *The Shariyat-Ki-Sugmad,* Book One, reads: "Dedicated to the ECK Masters of the Ancient Order of Vairagi, who waited patiently for the right time to give this message to the world." That the ECK Masters were patient is an understatement. After suffering excessive persecution in ancient times, the Vairagi Adepts decided to make ECK a secret teaching. And so in about 3000 B.C., under the guidance of the renowned ECK Master Gopal Das, the teachings of ECK were removed from the public arena.[1]

For the next five thousand years or so, the teachings of ECK would be veiled in mystery. All instruction was given by word of mouth, in small groups. It was no easy task for the seeker to discover the Living ECK Master.

Today the Mahanta, the Living ECK Master is making every effort to bring ECKANKAR back out to the whole world. It's almost as if he were trying to make up for lost time, for so many are hungry for the teachings of the Light and Sound of God, and some have waited lifetimes to once again find the path of ECK.

The Mahanta, the Living ECK Master faced resistance from some who wished ECKANKAR to remain veiled in mystery and secrecy. These people criticized his actions, saying he was trying to make ECKANKAR into an orthodox religion. What they forget is that ECKANKAR was never intended to be a secret teaching in the first place; it only became so as a last resort to protect it from the persecutions of an ancient priesthood.

An example of such resistance was when Sri Harold decided to bring the HU Chant, or HU Song, to the public. A number of chelas were upset about it. Yet in *The Shariyat-Ki-Sugmad,* Book Two, it is written, "The mantra of the HU was the sacred chant of all the people in the Satya Yuga."[2] The Satya Yuga was the first era of this creation, the Golden Age. The ECK Masters knew if the world was going to be able to move ahead in our time, the HU would need to be given to humanity once again.

This isn't to say ECKANKAR will no longer have its secret, or esoteric, side. But now the secret side will be where it more naturally belongs, on the inner spiritual planes.

If the ECK Masters had to wait patiently for five thousand years to go public again with the teachings of ECK, they have had to be even more patient to see a new Golden Wisdom Temple established. This is an event that happens at such rare intervals that it marks a giant step forward for the spiritual consciousness of the planet.

The timing of such occasions is critical. The spiritual currents of ECK stream out into the lower worlds, and like the tides of the oceans, they ebb and flow cyclically. The Mahanta was to show me some striking examples of how the spiritual hierarchy timed their work in harmony with these spiritual flows.

Sri Harold has often spoken of the importance of the Law of Economy in these lower worlds. This is the principle of getting the most advantage for your expended efforts. One doesn't become an ECK Master without mastering this important law. The principle of right timing is an important application of the Law of Economy.

*   *   *

In April 1990 I went to see a movie titled *For All Mankind.* It was the story of the years from 1968 to 1972 in the American space program, which climaxed in the missions to the moon. This was the glorious culmination of mankind's quest into space in the twentieth century.

I was a teenager during those years. Although I vividly recalled the excitement of the moon missions and the earlier Gemini flights beginning in 1965, I hadn't given any further thought to them since then. Sitting in the movie theater, the drama and wonder of those years began to come back. The span of time since it all happened gave a good perspective to these tumultuous events that coincided with the early years of ECKANKAR since 1965.

As I sat in the theater watching the film, I was struck how this great mission to the moon paralleled the Mahanta's mission to bring out the teachings of ECKANKAR.

For example, Paul Twitchell became the Mahanta in 1965 and began publicly launching the spiritual teachings of ECKANKAR into the world. He called them "The Ancient Science of Soul Travel." The Soviet and American astronauts did their first space walks in 1965. What a perfect outer reflection of Soul Travel this was: human beings liberated from the confines of the earth, walking freely above the world.

Another example: The first manned flight of the Apollo mission was completed on October 22, 1968, exactly as the ECK spiritual new year began. This signified to me that the cycle of space exploration upon which the human race was then embarking was a reflection of the spiritual exploration the Mahanta was leading.

The number nine, keyed to the high spiritual currents of the ECK, was very prominent in the Apollo missions to the moon. The first manned flight of the Lunar Module was named Apollo 9. The second flight would descend to within nine miles of the moon's surface. There would be a total of nine successful manned lunar flights, ending with Apollo 17.

The movie brought back to me many memories about those years in U.S. history: the riots, the protests, the war in Vietnam, and the assasinations of Dr. Martin Luther King, Jr. and Bobby Kennedy. The world went through a profound spiritual change.

The film reminded me how much humanity can accomplish when it sets high goals for itself. Not only did we succeed in going to the moon, but we did it a number of times.

As I left the theater, I got to wondering why our quest for the high frontier of space seemed to die after the last of the moon missions was over. It was as if the last flight completed a gestation and gave birth to a new world realization: we were part of the cosmos now.

Then it occurred to me that humanity's quest into outer space had turned inward. We had reached for the moon and touched it. This was the fulfillment of the outer dream. Then humanity began to turn within and reach for the spiritual dream. Critics in America would see only the seeming loss of interest in material ambitions. They couldn't understand the need for the inner quest.

As I left the theater, I wondered why this movie had been made now. Why, during the building of the Temple of ECK, was Hollywood putting before the public consciousness the memories of the moon mission and the years of 1968–72? Was the ECK behind this? Did the Mahanta want the public awareness to reconnect with those years at this time?

On my way home from the movie, I had a sudden urge to stop by a bookstore. It was late, and the store would be closing in about ten minutes. But I had learned not to ignore these little promptings from the ECK. As I walked into the store, I just started walking up and down the aisles. Suddenly a particular book seemed to jump out at me. It was titled simply *Cycles,* by Samuel A. Schreiner, Jr.[3] It sounded interesting, so I bought it and headed on home.

That night as I lay in bed I couldn't sleep because all the ideas of the movie and the years 1968–72 were bouncing around in my head. So I picked up my new book and idly flipped through the pages. Suddenly a passage jumped out at me. The author was describing the discoveries of one Dr. Landscheidt, an expert in the research of cycles.

The author wrote,

Dr. Landscheidt is the epitome of today's cycle thinker. It is, therefore, appropriate to give him the last word on cycle prophecy. His outline of history is based on what he calls instability events, periods of change and revolution that take place at the turning of cycles when "the special constellation of Sun and planets that makes the center of mass and the Sun's surface coalesce." To appreciate his look ahead, it's best to start with his description of two of these periods that most of us will recognize or recall.[4]

There follow descriptions of two periods in our century. The second was 1968–72! Schreiner quotes Dr. Landscheidt:

> About 1968 to 1972: Upheavals and rebellions of students all over the world; spread of hippies; cultural revolution in China; six-day Arab Israeli war; new economic structures in Czechoslovakia, suppressed by Russian invasion; turning point in Vietnam; space travel; astronauts on the Moon; Glomar Challenger expedition, plate tectonics; first AIDS infections; ecological movement; Gnostics of Princeton; Pop art.[5]

I put the book down to think a minute, for the ECK-Vidya was opening before me. Why was I being given these connections now, eighteeen years after the fact? I picked up my dream diary from the night before and was startled to see that I had scribbled down a dream about former President Richard Nixon. Nixon had been the U.S. president during the years 1969–74! What was going on here? I gave up all hope of falling asleep now. I've learned that when the ECK-Vidya opens, it is best to get all you can at that time before the window closes again.

I picked up the book on cycles and skimmed through it some more, wondering if anything else might jump out and catch my attention. Not to be disappointed, I found, four pages previous to what I had just read, a sketch of an important but little-known cycle. It was a cousin of the one that ran from 1968–72, but more rare and significant. I would later learn that this occurrence had happened only seven times in the past thirty-four hundred years. And when was this rare cycle to peak again? In April 1990. That was right now!

I could see where the Mahanta was leading us. I believe that in 1968–72 the world had gone on its vision quest to the moon. It had brought back the vision of Earth as part of the cosmos—not just in theory anymore. We had seen our fragile blue globe from far away, seen it rising over the lunar horizon. And all this had come as the Mahanta had given the world the vision of the inner worlds. Now the second step was occurring: Bringing the vision down to earth and applying it. Spiritually this meant the Temple of ECK, the grounding of mankind's vision.

ECKANKAR was known early on as the ancient science of Soul Travel because humanity had to travel through inner and outer space and catch the vision. But now ECKANKAR was becoming known as the religion of the Light and Sound of God. The word *religion* comes from a Latin root which means "to retie" or "refasten." In other words, to reconnect one thing to another. We needed to reconnect our inner and outer visions with the world right here.

Before moving ahead with this story, it is time to pause a minute and discuss the significance of cycles. Paul Twitchell's book *The ECK-Vidya, Ancient Science of Prophecy* is a study of this aspect of the teachings of ECKANKAR. In the first chapter of that book, Paul describes a visit he took to the temple ruins in Delphi, Greece, where people used to come from all over the ancient world for prophecy and advice from the oracle.

He relates how during that visit he began his practice of the ECK-Vidya, when a deep voice spoke to him, saying, "Beloved one, who in these times has been given wisdom to know and understand the gods are immortal, and still have power to grant those willing to listen the power of prophecy and wisdom, you will know and understand the future, past and present of all beings and things. This gift has been given to you now."[6]

Paul knew in a flash that this was the voice of Apollo, the divine god of Greece, upon whose ruins he stood. Apollo, after whom the moon missions were named. As Paul was bringing ECKANKAR out to the world, the world was moving out into space on the wings of Apollo. I was fortunate to visit those temple ruins myself in 1986. There I had a vision of Athena, the famous prophetess and guardian of ancient Athens, whose symbol was the owl.

Paul writes: "There is one great rule that goes in the ECK-Vidya. 'Whosoever, and whatsoever is born or done at a given moment of time has the qualities of that moment of time.'"[7] This key point encourages us to look at some of the qualities of the time of the building of the Temple of ECK. For these qualities define its nature and potential and will be as meaningful centuries from now as they are today.

The value of the understanding of cycles is knowing the right place and time to set plans in motion. Timing is critical and can often make the difference between success and failure of a project. Paul writes, "The doctrine of cycles contains much vital information and many amazing solutions to the philosophical problems that have puzzled the western students of spiritual matters for centuries. The accumulated wisdom of the ages has been employed in the formulation of this basic doctrine which constitutes the solid foundation of cosmic and planetary chronology. It was considered very sacred and esoteric and was guarded in the secret chambers of the temple of antiquity and only revealed to the high initiates at the time of initiation into the mysteries."[8]

One of the ECK Masters who taught in the secret

chambers of Greek antiquity was Pythagoras. He is credited with discovering the numerical ratios which are the underlying basis of the musical scale. But historians often discredit him for his claim to have also discovered the harmony of the spheres, a celestial symphony of sound that fills all space.

We in ECKANKAR know Pythagoras was talking about the Sound of God, or the ECK. To those who can't hear it, this music is pure fantasy. But the music of ECK is very real indeed. It is the heart of the teachings of ECK.

Now back to our story. Like Pythagoras before him, Dr. Landscheidt takes an interdisciplinary, holistic approach to the puzzles presented by the workings of the universe. The author of *Cycles* writes: "Computing intervals in the energy wave from the sun over a period stretching from 5259 B.C. to A.D. 2347, Dr. Landscheidt found mathematically consonant intervals equivalent to the major sixth (3:5) and minor sixth (5:8) in music emerging."[9]

In an analysis of the periodic alignment of Jupiter, the sun's center, and the solar system's center of mass, Dr. Landscheidt says, "The results presented here are a new substantiation of the Pythagorean harmony of the spheres."[10]

I finally put down the book *Cycles*. It was about 3:00 a.m. The ECK-Vidya had made one thing clear to me that night. I felt there was a very important connection between the building of the Temple of ECK and some rare cycle which was climaxing at that very time. I was willing to leave it at that. Whatever the connection was, further clues would have to wait until another day.

But I didn't have to wait long. Pretty soon the Mahanta began to put some odd-shaped puzzle pieces into my hands. With each puzzle piece I thought, What am I supposed to do with this? Where does it fit in? But the ECK-Vidya wouldn't let up. It kept giving me things as fast as I could absorb them.

The first key puzzle piece came when I was rereading the book *Difficulties of Becoming the Living ECK Master,* by Paul Twitchell. I came across this passage on pages 251–52:

> During the early part of the seventeenth century, four ECK spiritual masters who serve in the spiritual hierarchy, met in the ancient sacred city of Agam Des in the Himalayan Mountains. They were: Ramaj, viceroy for Sat Nam, the great deity of the fifth world, commonly called the Soul Plane; Rebazar Tarzs, emissary for ECK in this physical universe today; Gopal Das, spiritual master at the Golden Wisdom Temple on the Astral plane and Yaubl Sacabi, spiritual head of the ancient city of Agam Des.
>
> They met to discuss the birth of the coming avatar for the twentieth century, Peddar Zaskq.[11]

This historic meeting would mark the first step toward the establishment of the modern movement of ECKANKAR and the Temple of ECK.

The second puzzle piece came to me when I was listening to the audiocassette of Sri Harold's talk "The Story of Paul Twitchell," from the 1984 ECKANKAR International Youth Conference. In that talk Sri Harold explained how Peddar Zaskq was born in his previous life in 1811 near New Madrid, Missouri. At the time of his birth there occurred a series of powerful earthquakes that shook the entire eastern part of the United States. The quakes were among the most powerful ever noted in North America. Sri Harold explained that this was the beginning of Paul Twitchell's previous life as Peddar Zaskq, as recorded in Paul's book *The Drums of ECK*.

While the meeting in Agam Des in the early seventeenth century marked the first step of bringing ECKANKAR out into the world again, the birth of Peddar Zaskq in 1811 marked the second major step. It was a sort of world ground-breaking ceremony and preparation for the advent of this Living ECK Master's appearance in the twentieth century.

The third puzzle piece was the Temple of ECK itself, built between 1989 and 1990, a major milestone in solidly establishing the teachings of ECKANKAR once again in this world.

I kept kicking these three dates around in my mind: the early 1600s, 1811, and 1989. Around this time I took another trip down to the bookstore in hopes of finding something interesting to read. Since I was thinking a lot about cycles, I thought to pick up another book on the subject. A new book had just come out called *Tables of Planetary Phenomena* by Neil F. Michelsen.[12] I was flipping through it just out of curiosity when I came across a chart that had these dates: 1632, 1811, 1989!

In explaining the linking of these dates, the author wrote, "This is a rare event and has happened only seven times in the last 3400 years! We are in such a period now which started April 28, 1989, and will last through December 23, 1990."[13]

Instantly I realized this was one of the cycles that I'd read about in the book *Cycles*. The current expression of this cosmic cycle started less than a month before ECKANKAR acquired permission to build the Temple of ECK on May 22, 1989 and ended just a few months after the Temple Dedication on October 22, 1990. Hence the building of the Temple of ECK was neatly enfolded within the cycle. I was sure now that the Mahanta was leading me to something.

It is worth a few paragraphs to explain what this cycle is. Most people believe the center of our solar system is the sun. But the mass of the planets pulls the system center away from the sun's center. Therefore, not only the planets but the sun itself all rotate about a point in space that is the actual center of the whole system. The distance between the sun's center and this actual center of the whole solar system can vary from almost nothing up to more than 850,000 miles.

It is very rare when the two centers come together. At that time there is a balancing of the whole solar system. This phenomenon is what took place during the building of the Temple of ECK in 1989. It also took place in 1811, in 1632, and four other times in the past thirty-four hundred years.

Neil Michelsen writes:

The last two times this happened was in 1810–12 and 1632–33. Weather and climate after 1810 were more extreme than anything ever experienced since. 1816 was the year without a summer when the northeastern US and western Europe had freezing weather every month of the year. A succession of cold summers and short growing seasons triggered famines in places such as Switzerland and the Ukraine. J.D. Post in the *Journal of Interdisciplinary History* (1973) said: "The years 1812–1817 introduced three decades of economic pause punctuated by recurring crises, distress, social upheaval, international migrations, political rebellion and pandemic disease."

The climate of the 1630s and 40s was also extreme. The River Thames froze solid during this time and the people of London held "frost fairs" on the ice. This had not happened for at least 150 years. There were also short growing seasons, and the winter of 1641 was one of the three worst in the entire century for the American colonies. Also, this period had one of the most intensive concentrations of volcanic activity of the past 500 years.[14]

What isn't so easy for historians to see in those eras is the spiritual progress that was going on behind all the chaos. When the wind of Divine Spirit begins to blow, the pace of world karma picks up as a cleansing takes place. The same can be seen happening today. The media focus on the problems which seem to be overtaking civilization, while missing the underlying spiritual transformation.

So I began to see the analogy here: I believe when the solar system is centered, balanced within itself, the forces of ECK can more easily pour forth. Such propitious cosmic alignments are taken advantage of by the spiritual hierarchy. According to the Law of Economy, they take advantage of the times and seasons which will best benefit their mission. So I believe the scope of the Mahanta's mission and the Temple of ECK extended far out beyond the periphery of our planet into the cosmos.

I wasn't totally satisfied with what the Mahanta had shown me here. To me the grand plan of the Mahanta was a romantic drama and shouldn't be related to celestial mechanics. But a few days after being shown all of this, I came across a remarkable passage in Paul Twitchell's Wisdom Note of August 1971, written a month before he died:

> The Mahanta comes because of the Sugmad's love for Its creation and because without the coming, the creation could not survive

self-destruction from the negative imbalance. This periodic drama is played out at intervals and *while it is romantic in nature, or man's view of it, it is also mechanical and impersonal* [italics mine] in the sense that it must occur to sustain the creation.[15]

There is one more point I'd like to make about this great periodic balancing of our solar system. It is a fascinating connection to the fact that Paul Twitchell was the 971st Mahanta. This phenomenon had been occurring at approximately 179-year intervals. It happened in 55 B.C. It happened again 179 years later in 124 A.D., 179 years after that in 303 A.D., and 179 years after that in 482 A.D. But then the cycle missed a beat.

After another 179 years, in 661 A.D., during the Dark Ages of earth's modern history, no balancing took place. A long period followed until 971 years later, when the cycle reestablished itself in 1632 A.D.[16] As noted above, it was during the early part of the seventeenth century that the historic meeting occurred in Agam Des where the ECK Masters met to discuss the birth of the 971st Avatar, or Mahanta. Then 179 years later in 1811–12, the great New Madrid earthquakes shook America as Peddar Zaskq was born. And 179 years after 1811 brings us to 1989 and building the Temple of ECK.

I mentioned before that the current cycle of solar system balancing took place from April 1989 to December 1990. The time when this balancing was most exact in this period was in April 1990. That is the month the Mahanta showed me all of the insights in this chapter.

The 971st Mahanta, Paul Twitchell, completed his mission in the 971st year of our millennium—he translated, or died, on September 17, 1971 (9/17/71). With our limited human knowledge we can only stand in awe of the cosmic order of the universe. But I hope this chapter helps us see that the spiritual and physical universes are interwoven with consummate skill by the golden thread of ECK, the Light and Sound of God. The Law of Balance and Law of Economy blend into the Law of Love. Nothing is left to chance, and yet there is perfect freedom for all. The same immutable spiritual laws that uphold the universes are at work in the smallest concerns of our everyday lives.

9

Vision Quest Two
The Holy Fire of ECK

The Living ECK Master always brings Light and Love into the world so that all men shall profit by them. Not just his own followers, but the world of itself. Each of those who follow him should be caught up in the fire of his love. This love begins in each like a tiny flame then begins to consume them until they love all because it is life, and life is God.

This is known as the holy fire.

—*The Shariyat-Ki-Sugmad,* Book One

In early 1989, I began having a series of dreams about an Eighth Initiate in ECKANKAR. I knew he was a member of the ECK Spiritual Council and one of Paul Twitchell's first students. In early spring I read he was to be the guest speaker at the Oregon regional seminar. On the Friday the seminar was to begin, I joined a friend to drive the sixty miles. As we traveled, I thought about this Eighth Initiate and felt he had something special to share with us.

The seminar was held in a hotel in Eugene, Oregon. I went to a number of talks, workshops, and roundtable discussions. But it seems wherever I went, I kept bumping into this man. When the evening session of the seminar arrived and the MC introduced Elmo DeWhitt as the guest speaker, I was on the edge of my chair. I didn't want to miss a word of his talk, for the ECK-Vidya kept telling me he would say something that would be very important.

Elmo gave a very interesting talk, spiced with many stories, each illustrating the way Divine Spirit works in our daily lives. Then he branched off into a different subject. He spoke of a lunch he had shared with the Living ECK Master and some of the conversation they had had together. He said: "Harold told me that Paul's mission had been to bring ECKANKAR up to Consciousness Five and his [Sri Harold's] mission was to bring it up to Consciousness Nine."

This statement hit me like a bolt of lightning. The speaker turned to other topics, but I couldn't take my thoughts off that last statement. I felt the implications for ECKANKAR and for the world were simply earthshaking. To appreciate the significance of it requires a little background history. Paul Twitchell wrote the following prophecy in September 1971 just before he died:

> As October 22 draws near, the whole movement, the Outer Works approaches what will be known as CONSCIOUSNESS FIVE. The past year has been a difficult one for many, for the movement as a whole. In a way of speaking, we have passed through the foetal stage, this past year was one of labour and delivery. October 22 of this year will ring in the birth of CONSCIOUSNESS FIVE and heralds the explosion of the teachings of ECK into the mainstream of the Earth's Twentieth Century Civilization. We will have much to celebrate and much to do, Beloved Ones.[1]

Consciousness Five was a phrase Paul coined to denote the spiritual awareness of Self-Realization, which occurs on the Fifth Plane. In September 1971 there were little more than a handful of ECKists who had reached this initiation. Yet Paul tells us the movement as a whole would reach that level on October 22, 1971.

To grasp the depth of what Paul wrote requires the understanding of a whole new dimension of spiritual thought—that which deals with initiations and expansions of consciousness *within a group.* Much has been written and discussed over the centuries about individual initiation, individual attainment, and individual spiritual liberation. But humanity's understanding of the spiritual laws pertaining to group service and group attainment is much more primitive.

For example, what would it mean to a Second Initiate to be part of a group which, as a whole, was expressing Consciousness Five? How many initiates having Consciousness Five does it take in a group for the whole group to be a channel for Consciousness Five? What significance does such a group attainment have for the world as a whole? Just as the achievement of an individual has, down the ages, served to uplift the human race, so a similar group achievement should serve to uplift humanity even more rapidly.

As I see it, one consequence of Consciousness Five in ECKANKAR was that all the initiations were lifted to a higher level. A Fifth Initiate of a thousand years ago might only be a First Initiate today because the whole human race has evolved to a much higher state of consciousness. This continual forward movement of humanity creates a periodic need for a new religious dispensation to present the ancient truths in an updated form. This is one mission of the Mahanta.

For a movement as a whole to be a channel for Consciousness Five was revolutionary. Down through history, individual initiates had reached Consciousness Five, one by one, as they unfolded spiritually. But in 1971, the entire outer works of ECKANKAR would attain this level. And if one looks at what the world went through during the years of Paul's term as the Mahanta from 1965–71, it is easy to see how this spread out into society.

Yet here was Sri Harold telling this Eighth Initiate that the Mahanta would take the movement of ECKANKAR far beyond Consciousness Five to Consciousness Nine, which corresponds to the first plane of God-Realization. If the group effects of Consciousness Five had been difficult to fathom, the consequences of Consciousness Nine would be much more so. For this state of consciousness is attained by very few indeed at any given time in history.

It must have taken the human race hundreds of millennia before a group of people could become a collective channel for the Fifth-Plane energies of Divine Spirit. Yet the ECK was moving us along so fast that eighteen years after Consciousness Five It was already leading us on toward Consciousness Nine.

After the seminar, I went home with the Sound of ECK buzzing in my ears. The demands of work and family soon put my feet back on the ground. But I didn't forget that special talk.

Around this time, another Eighth Initiate in ECKANKAR suggested that groups of ECKists get together and do something challenging, such as climb a mountain. The idea was to build a strong trust and bond of brotherhood and teamwork. I got the idea to organize a vision quest for the Higher Initiates in Oregon. My plan was for us to meet somewhere up in

104

the mountains and try to catch a vision of the Mahanta's mission. I asked the Regional ECK Spiritual Aide for Oregon about it, and he had no objections.

I spent a few days pondering on a good title for the vision quest. My initial title was "A Vision of Consciousness Nine." I held that phrase in my thoughts for a few days and all sorts of unusual things happened. For example, I went to an ECK Worship Service and a friend who knew nothing about the plans for the vision quest came up to me. She said, "I just felt I had to give you this book! I don't know why." The title of the book was *Living with Vision: Reclaiming the Power of the Heart.*

Another special experience came through the ECK-Vidya during that week. I was doing what is called the Shariyat technique. In this spiritual exercise, one asks a question of the Mahanta, then opens the scriptures of ECKANKAR, *The Shariyat-Ki-Sugmad,* at random. What is found on that page will be the contemplation seed for the answer to the question.

The first time I did this, I used Book One of *The Shariyat.* The question was, What should be the purpose of the vision quest? When I opened *The Shariyat* at random, it fell open to the first page of chapter 9, titled "Visions of the SUGMAD"!

I tried the exercise again a few days later. This time I used Book Two of *The Shariyat.* The question was the same as the first time: What should be the purpose of the vision quest? To my amazement the page I opened to was again the first page of chapter 9, which in Book Two of *The Shariyat* is titled "The Visions of Lai Tsi." I had never noticed before that chapter 9 of both books of *The Shariyat-Ki-Sugmad* were about spiritual visions.

The ninth chapter of Book One of *The Shariyat* had a passage which would serve as the basis for the vision quest:

The forms of divine life in the universe break forth from the seer as vision, from the mystic as Light, and in the ECK initiates up to the Fourth Circle as Sound. But the Mahdis, the Initiates of the Fifth Circle, have vision, Light, and Sound. The higher each goes on the planes of the worlds of true Spirit, the greater the vision, Light, and Sound become.[2]

The title I finally settled on for the vision quest was "Visions of the SUGMAD." This phrase can be understood two ways. It can mean *our* visions of the SUGMAD. It can also mean the SUGMAD's own visions.

Once a theme was given to the vision quest, invitations were printed and sent out to all the Higher Initiates in Oregon. The date for the vision quest was set for August 25, 1990. The place was a site in the remote Oregon mountains where I had heard Native Americans used to do their own vision quests.

A few days after the invitations were sent out, the Mahanta gave me another significant ECK-Vidya experience. This one harkened back to the initial dream recorded in chapter 3. In that dream I had had a life-changing encounter with a spiritual being in the form of a white owl, while I was on a vision quest as a Chippewa Indian. This had been my symbolic vision of the Temple of ECK.

What occurred happened on June 21, 1990. That night I had the following dream: I am Soul traveling through the mountains of Oregon and go to the site of the vision quest. The famed ECK Master Milarepa is waiting there. Pointing into the night sky he says, "Look!" In the sky I see a formation of white birds flying down toward us. When they come close I see they are ten white owls. They hover above us in a triangular formation. Milarepa says, "They are here on planet Earth for an important mission. You must learn from them what you can."

I awoke and wrote this dream down in my journal with great excitement. I saw it as a strong confirmation for me that the coming vision quest was in line with the mission of the Mahanta.

The next Sunday, I needed to travel to the Oregon coast to serve as a facilitator for an ECK Worship Service. While there I was a guest at the house of a dear friend and Higher Initiate in ECK, whom we'll call Frank.

When I got to Frank's house, he said he wanted to tell me about a very unusual dream he'd had the night of June 21.

"Please do!" I said.

"I had a vision of some sort of pyramid or mountain. On top of the mountain were ten owls. I didn't know what the vision meant, except that it was important."

I shared with him my own dream of ten owls on a mountaintop. We talked for over an hour about what it all meant and what it might mean for the vision quest and the Mahanta's mission. Later, when I arrived home and had time to read the newspaper, the headline was about how the northern spotted owl had been declared a threatened species. This happened on June 22, 1990.

That the northern spotted owl was declared a threatened species the day after Frank and I had our owl visions was a startling development to me. Until that time I had not thought of any possible connection between the Mahanta's mission and the environment. This would become more clear to me later.

*   *   *

The most provocative series of waking dreams I have ever experienced began to manifest after I had sent out the invitations to the vision quest. They began one night in a dream. In this dream, I had gone to inspect the site where the vision quest was to be held. When I got there, I was shocked to find the entire area had been burned to the ground by a great forest fire. Only one small island of green remained in a vast landscape of smoldering mountains. It was a little grassy knoll. In the center of the knoll was a little cabin, and in the cabin was sitting a Brother of the Leaf, a Higher Initiate in ECK, playing a flute. The cabin had a single telephone line that ran down the mountain to the valley below. As the flute player made his beautiful music, the phone line would carry his melody down the mountain. It was miraculous that the phone line had not been destroyed by the fire.

When I awoke from this dream, I felt a strange mixture of alarm and wonder. The feeling of alarm came from a real concern that a forest fire might actually be coming to that area. Forest fires in August are not unusual in Oregon. Yet the symbology of the flute player held great promise. In my dream diary the next day I interpreted the dream like this:

> The great forest fire is symbolic of the Holy Fire of ECK as it sweeps into the lower worlds, cleansing all in its path. The island of green represents the higher worlds. The flute player signifies the Soul Plane, for the sound of the flute is the Sound of the ECK on that plane. The phone line which brings the sound of the flute to the valley below is the indestructible link of Light

and Sound that links together all life through the ECK.

I kept this dream to myself, not even sharing it with my family. A few days later, I traveled to the vision-quest site with my family. I wanted to check everything out, so I could advise anyone who came what to bring and what to expect, plus to draw up a good map of how to get there. My wife and two children hiked with me up the trail about a mile. They stayed to enjoy a waterfall, while I went on ahead the remaining half-mile by myself.

Upon my return, the Holy Fire theme occurred again. My five-year-old daughter saw me coming down the trail. She ran up to me and said, "Daddy, you're on fire!" I stopped in my tracks and looked at her. "Why did you say that, Tolly?" I asked her. "Oh, I don't know," she laughed, and that was the end of the conversation as far as she was concerned.

The vision quest, as mentioned before, was to be held on August 25. The weekend of August 3 was the annual Oregon ECKANKAR Campout. This was held that year by Paulina Lake at Newberry Volcano in central Oregon. It would prove to be a momentous weekend for Oregon and for the world.

My family and I arrived at the campout Friday evening. As soon as we got unpacked and set up camp, I spotted my good friend Frank, who had shared my vision of ten owls. I walked over to him, and we sat down to talk. The first thing he asked me really took me by surprise. "Have you been experiencing any strong fire themes in your life lately?" I said yes, I had. Why did he ask?

Frank explained that he and another chela were organizing an upcoming ECKANKAR seminar for the chelas in the state. The title was to be "The Holy Fire of ECK." Frank said, "Last night I dreamed that my inner house burned down. It was a little unsettling." I shared with him some of my recent experiences with the inner fire.

That evening a series of lightning storms began hitting central Oregon, especially around the area of our campout at Paulina Lake. By Saturday, news filtered in that the fires were raging out of control and our campground might have to be evacuated. Meanwhile, someone mentioned that Iraq had invaded the wealthy oil sheikhdom of Kuwait, setting off an international alarm for the safety of the world's oil supply.

But our campout continued, despite the alarming news from the state and world media. The ECK-Vidya spoke to me many times that weekend, giving subtle insights on what was unfolding. I knew intuitively that the Holy Fire of ECK was sweeping the world. As the Temple of ECK took physical form, it was drawing forth the spiritual energies in a way not experienced before on earth.

No matter where you are, the ECK, Divine Spirit, can speak to you about the significance of what is happening at the time, whether in your own personal life or in international affairs. On three separate occasions that Saturday, the Golden-tongued Wisdom gave me the same message. Someone would walk up to me, show me a pine cone from a bristlecone pine tree, and say, "Did you know that the seeds of the bristlecone pine can only sprout after the cone has been burned?"

It seemed to me that the ECK was telling me that the living tree (the teachings of ECKANKAR) could reseed the earth only if the Holy Fire of ECK first burned away the old debris. This insight was helpful in understanding the karmic repercussions that swept

110

the world that weekend with the invasion of Kuwait by Iraq.

By Sunday it was apparent that the camping area we were in was nearly surrounded by fire, and park officials asked everyone to leave as soon as possible. Many of us were forced to take wide detours to get home. Later in the week newspapers reported that the fires which burned throughout Oregon that weekend were some of the worst in the history of the central Oregon region.

A parallel to this on the world level was set in motion by the invasion of Kuwait that weekend. When Iraqi forces were finally driven from Kuwait in 1991, they would leave behind hundreds of oil wells set afire. These would prove to be the some of the worst sets of fires known in human history.

The weeks between the Oregon campout and the vision quest on August 25 became an almost continual expression of fire themes in my personal life. I could well relate to something Sri Harold once said: "The ECK works through me to show the ECK-Vidya constantly. Sometimes there is no rest, no peace."[3]

On the evening of August 24, the eve of the vision quest, I told my wife, "I'm so tired of all the fire themes. I just want to forget about it. I'm going to the video store and just rent any old movie to take my mind off everything."

So I drove to the neighborhood video-rental store to pick up a videocassette. Since I didn't care which movie it was, I just went to the beginning of the row. The tapes were arranged alphabetically, and I picked up a movie called *Always,* starring Richard Dreyfus. When I got home and put it on to play, I groaned with dismay. It was movie about a forest-fire fighter. "Do I have to watch this?" I asked the Mahanta, the Inner

111

Master. "Can't I have just one evening without any more Holy Fire symbolism?" But I settled down to watch, bracing myself for another dissertation by the ECK on the subtleties of the Holy Fire.

It wasn't long into the movie that I realized it was no ordinary film. In fact, the whole story was a beautiful statement about love, service, and spiritual awakening. I sat upright in my chair when a certain scene occurred, for it was a near-perfect reflection of the dream in which I had gone to inspect the vision-quest site and had found it all burned up except a small green area.

The hero of the movie had just died when his fire-fighting airplane crashed into the trees. He left his body and found himself at a little island of green grass in a landscape of burned mountains. There he met a spirit guide, played by Audrey Hepburn. He had to face himself and the record of his life to see whether he was worthy of love.

The movie was a wonderful story of how a man found his vision and was touched by the Holy Fire of ECK, which is divine love. There probably wasn't a movie on the planet that could have more perfectly expressed the theme and tenor of the moment. I saw it as a promise from the Mahanta that the vision quest would open a wider channel of love and service in all of those attending.

The day of the vision quest finally arrived. I picked up four other Brothers of the Leaf, and we headed south for the three-and-a-half-hour trip. As we drove along, we shared our thoughts and feelings of the past few days. I was very concerned about the possibility of a forest fire, especially after the fires at the Oregon campout. We all agreed that under no circumstances would any of us light a fire!

I wasn't sure how many H.I.'s would show up. Going on a vision quest sounded interesting in theory. But the more people thought about staying up all night on a dark, cold mountain in the forest, the less interesting they thought it was. We arrived at the trailhead parking lot in the evening; a local ECKist had generously agreed to watch our cars during the night.

By the time the sun had set, everyone was up at the vision-quest site. I counted heads, and there were ten of us. I mused to myself, Here we are, ten owls on a mountaintop.

One reason I had chosen late August for the vision quest was that the chance of rain was negligible. But as darkness fell, rain clouds were gathering. Instead of disappointment I felt relief, for the moisture would reduce the fire danger.

That night the ten of us talked, laughed, contemplated, napped, shivered, told stories, and sang the HU. We huddled under a small tarp as a gentle rain fell most of the night. At times we were as one. At other times, each went to a quiet place to search for his or her own vision. Since none of us had expected wet weather, we had to improvise rain gear from plastic garbage bags. At one point, as we stood clothed in garbage bags, laughing at each other, someone asked what the waking dream of *that* was. Fortunately, no one ventured an interpretation!

Several weeks before the vision quest, I had asked one of the Higher Initiates to prepare a group contemplation for us. She was inspired to choose the theme "A Vision of Consciousness Nine." I had originally intended to use just that title for the vision quest itself but had decided not to at the last minute. That this other Higher Initiate ended up choosing the exact same title for her group contemplation was to me another confirmation from the Mahanta of this aspect of his mission.

When dawn finally came, most of us were eager to be off the mountain and get a good, hot breakfast. But as I wound my way down the trail, I felt a little disappointed. After all the buildup of the previous months, I had expected some grand vision. It hadn't come. Disillusionment settled over me, and I wondered whether the whole vision quest wasn't a waste of time after all. When I shared my feelings with the Regional ECK Spiritual Aide, he encouraged me to take time to digest the experience and get some perspective on it.

It was sage counsel. The ECK will rarely grant us visions at the time we expect them. Had I been more inventive, I should have guessed a "Vision of Consciousness Nine" would come on a date made up of several nines, like 9-9-90. And lo, it did come on that date.

But before I share that vision, I wish to make a disclaimer. My vision was not an *experience* of Consciousness Nine. It was a statement of the impact this consciousness would have on ECKANKAR and on the world. I have not personally been privileged to experience Consciousness Nine. But as ECKANKAR moves into Consciousness Nine, all of us will be affected, no matter what our level of growth or understanding. And to me this is what the vision was really about.

The vision came in a dream: Two friends and I are sitting on a hill, looking out over a river valley. We are waiting expectantly for something important. Gradually, the sun rises in the east. As it crests the horizon, thunder and lightning shake the atmosphere. The higher the sun rises, the louder the thunder and the brighter the lightning. When the sun reaches its zenith, it stops. A voice whispers, "This is Consciousness Five."

Then a second sun dawns in the east. Its birth is attended by a massive rolling thunder and sheets of flashing lightning. As this second sun gradually ascends into the sky, the thunder and lightning crackle and boom louder and brighter, building in a rising crescendo of magnificent Light and Sound until the whole atmosphere is pulsing and vibrating with it. As the second sun nears the first, the Sound becomes almost deafening and the Light shoots out in torrents of electric energy in all directions.

We three witnesses stand awestruck at the display unfolding before us. Then, in a titanic explosion which rocks the very foundation of the world, the second sun eclipses the first and shoots into a higher orbit. This time the voice whispers, "Consciousness Nine."

When I awoke from this dream, I didn't even bother to write it down in my dream journal. It was unforgettably seared into my brain. It seemed to me that Consciousness Five had taken ECKANKAR as far as it could go. It was time for Consciousness Nine to launch ECKANKAR into a newer and higher orbit.

There is a paradox in this. On one hand the Mahanta is doing everything possible to bring ECKANKAR down from the mountaintop. He has put it into simpler language. He is shaping the teachings into a more accessible structure so people can more easily relate to them. Yet on the other hand he is boosting ECKANKAR to a higher level than it has ever been before in history. This is the inner side of his mission that I believe many people have overlooked.

What is the solution to this paradox? The closer Soul gets to the divine, the simpler things become.

Soul begins to realize that God is love, or more simply yet, God is!

So perhaps there is no paradox after all.

* * *

The Dream Weaver continued to weave in the significant events in my personal life with significant events of the Temple of ECK. The permission to build the Temple of ECK had come on May 22, my wedding anniversary. The Temple ground breaking had come at 10:30 a.m. on September 11, 1989, the same day, hour, and minute that I began a new career. October 12, the day the Temple was officially completed, was the first birthday of my second child, who was born during the building of the Temple.

The dedication ceremony for the new Temple of ECK was scheduled for October 22, 1990. On the night of October 21 I found myself at the Chanhassen Temple on the inner planes. Sri Harold was leading ten or twelve ECKists in a discussion class on the Shariyat-Ki-Sugmad. I had the impression that this was a brand-new volume of the Shariyat written by the ECK Masters expressly for the new Temple of ECK.

Each of us would read a paragraph from the Shariyat, using that paragraph as a lead-in to discuss what our personal missions were for the coming year. As each took a turn reading, it was fascinating to see how our missions were tied in with the reading. The first to read was a computer-systems analyst. He gave a presentation on a new computer system he was designing for the ECKANKAR Office. Sri Harold complimented him on his thoroughness and completeness.

The next person read a very interesting passage from the inner Shariyat: "On rare occasions, the

SUGMAD ITSELF moves forward. When IT does, the whole of creation is affected. The building of the Temple of ECK is planet earth's response to such a move forward." The ECKist who read this exclaimed, "Now that's a deep thought!" Sri Harold said, "Yes, it is."

Next it was my turn. My passage read: "The torch of the Vahana is lit from the Holy Fire, which burns in the Temple of ECK." I looked at Sri Harold and said, "So this is the culmination of the Holy Fire of ECK theme." He said, "I want you to write a report on this theme and present it to the ECKists." This chapter is my report to the ECKists.

So on October 22, 1990, one of the brightest days in the spiritual history of the human race, I closed a wondrous chapter in my life and opened a new one. At the time, I thought there was nothing that could ever compare to the experiences I'd had during the building of the Temple of ECK. I thought the Dream Weaver was finished with his tapestry. Not so!

The perfect conclusion to this chapter for me occurred in a waking dream on Monday, October 22, the day of the Temple dedication. It was the Dream Weaver's artful way of tying the last knot in this chapter.

Recall the story of the Oregon ECKANKAR campout at Newberry Volcano discussed earlier in this chapter. It had been held on the weekend of August 4–5. That had been the weekend I perceived so many waking dreams of the Holy Fire sweeping across the world, symbolically igniting the flames of physical forest fires all around us. It was two days after Iraq invaded Kuwait.

On October 22, the United States Senate voted to make Newberry Volcano a national monument![4] When I read this in the newspaper on Tuesday morning, I

117

thought, This is perfect. The political leadership of America, by this act of Congress, is acknowledging my Holy-Fire waking dreams. Of course they don't know it—but that doesn't matter.

This concludes my "report to the ECKists" on the theme of the Holy Fire of ECK.

10

Global Initiation

Today man is in the midst of the greatest
spiritual evolution known in the history of world
civilizations.

Civilization, too, is on the brink of a world
change. But this change is for the good of all
mankind. It will open the channels to God in such
a wide stream that I doubt if man will know or
recognize them.

—Paul Twitchell,
Dialogues with the Master

Everywhere people are discussing world changes.
Environmentalists stress the urgency of halting
the destruction of nature. Politicians grapple with problems that can no longer be defined by national borders.
Businesses struggle to adapt to a global economy.
Alarmists and fanatics preach a message of doom,
competing with the hopeful visions of new-agers and
futurists. Perhaps never before has history reached
such a point of climactic tension.

Charles Dickens's opening words to his novel on the
French Revolution, *A Tale of Two Cities,* are even more

119

apt today than they were some two hundred years ago: "It was the best of times, it was the worst of times." I believe the tumultuous surface events of our times are carried along by deep spiritual currents. These are the currents of ECK, of Divine Spirit, which unfold the human race over millions of years. When the cumulative unfoldment has reached a point of sufficient tension, it is time for humanity to step upward into a newer and higher state of consciousness.

I see these steps up in consciousness as global initiations. They may happen but once in many thousands or even tens of thousands of years. When they do, the Mahanta, the Living ECK Master and the spiritual hierarchy are especially active in the world. Anyone who is fortunate to be on earth at such times and is awake to the spiritual opportunities is indeed blessed. The opportunities for spiritual progress and service are unprecedented, not to mention the privilege of witnessing the transformation of the world!

But what is initiation? And what does it mean when applied on a global level? For an individual in ECKANKAR, an initiation is a linkup with the Light and Sound of God through the Mahanta, the Living ECK Master. It is an expansion of consciousness, an increase in responsibility, and a greater capacity to love and to serve all life. It is a gateway to a higher spiritual plane and deeper spiritual mysteries.

From my point of view, there are three main stages in an initiation cycle. First, there is a period of trial and testing. This serves the dual purpose of strengthening the candidate and seeing if he is worthy of the impending initiation. The tests of each initiation are different, for new laws must be mastered on each plane. Much karma is worked out at this time. And though the burden may be heavy, the growth is rapid.

Once the tests are passed, the second stage of the initiation occurs. This is the moment when the initiate is met by the Mahanta in an initiation ceremony. The Mahanta confers a secret spiritual word, or mantra, and a greater portion of the Light and Sound of God. At this time, the initiate will often experience a period of euphoria and spiritual lightness. His consciousness is opened wider than ever before, as is the heart center, and he sees the vision of the possibilities ahead of him. He feels many of his old problems are behind him for good. But really this is just a grace period.

Next comes the third stage of the initiation cycle. The clarity of the vision seems to fade, and the heart center can contract as many of the individual's old problems reappear. This morning-after syndrome can be a discouraging one. Now the initiate must go to work and find a way to settle into his newer and higher state of consciousness. He has a whole new set of laws and principles to master. He must redouble his efforts at the spiritual exercises. Then, over a period of months and years, he grows into the fullness of the initiation. His initial vision gradually becomes a reality.

If we compare these three main stages of initiation to humanity as a whole, we can better appreciate the state of the world and what it means.

First comes the period of testing. With each passing decade of the twentieth century, humanity faced greater and more difficult problems. I believe World Wars I and II cleared away vast amounts of world karma and broke up a lot of old and rigid states of consciousness. It seems to me that the blows of these wars softened the heart center of the human race and robbed war of much of its aura of glory. I feel the wars also brought a greater humility, as many people realized that the march of technical progress had not been paralleled by an equally rapid spiritual progress.

During the fifties many nations tried to return to the old games of greed and power. Suspicion and mistrust gave rise to the Iron Curtain and the Cold War. Tension increased until the world lived in fear of a nuclear war that would destroy civilization.

Then in the sixties, Paul Twitchell, the 971st Mahanta, the Living ECK Master brought the teachings of ECKANKAR out to the world. This shook up the negative patterns that had settled into place since the end of World War II.

From 1965 on, the spiritual awareness of humanity grew by leaps and bounds. Each passing year saw more and more people accept the spiritual truths which Paul Twitchell had brought to the world. Such ideas as Soul Travel, which were laughed at in the early sixties, were able to be more widely discussed and accepted by the eighties.

Many people awoke to the emerging crisis in the environment. A growing tide of public opinion demanded we take responsibility for our planet so that future generations would also be able to enjoy it.

The two great superpowers suffered loss of face during the period of the sixties, seventies, and eighties. America stumbled in Vietnam and the Soviet Union in Afghanistan. Both nations went home a little humbler and perhaps a little wiser.

The second phase of the global initiation cycle, the initiation itself, came during the building of the Temple of ECK. Sri Harold gave the secret word of HU to the whole human race, as he named 1990 the Year of the HU. The Iron Curtain collapsed. People danced on the Berlin Wall, and for a few wonderful months the world enjoyed its euphoria. People spoke glowingly of the dawn of a new age. Many politicians were ready to cash in on the peace dividend and convert their military budgets to solving the world's problems.

At the 1990 ECK Springtime Seminar in San Francisco, Sri Harold spoke of the global initiation which was upon us. He said that as the Berlin Wall crumbles and the Temple of ECK rises, earth is on the threshold of a global initiation. Mankind's attempt to move toward the Third, or Causal, Initiation, he noted, could be seen in the growing understanding of cause and effect and the international concern for the environment.

But alas, the shining vision beheld in 1989 seems now a little tarnished, and the euphoria has largely disappeared. Old ethnic rivalries have resurfaced in Europe and across the crumbling Soviet empire. Former communist nations struggle to survive the shift to market economies. The bad news of environmental degradation keeps coming in from all quarters. The United States has become mired in a stagnant economy, racial tensions, and urban decay.

Will humanity be able to attain the Causal Plane? Many of the old Astral-Plane attachments still hold us down. As Sri Harold wrote in the fall of 1990:

> For now, earth remains at the Second Initiation. Its group consciousness is largely grappling with its emotions. However, a growing vanguard of people is nearing the Third, or Causal, Initiation.
>
> It's too soon to tell about the planet karma. The group consciousness of earth has free will: It can decide whether to progress spiritually or not. If it does, then you'll see the concern over pollutants and individual freedom continue to grow. Otherwise, nations will go back to large-scale or pocket warfare to settle differences.

The Temple of ECK marks the dividing line between the Second and Third levels of mankind's group consciousness. The Vairagi Adepts want the Temple because mankind must soon move forward spiritually.

So the ECK Temple is here to help uplift the human race.[1]

The greatest strength any initiate has to carry him forward is the chanting of his secret word and the practice of the Spiritual Exercises of ECK. This is why I feel it is critical to spread the word of HU and the knowledge of the Spiritual Exercises of ECK to the world. If the collective initiate called humanity sings the HU, all over the world, it can make the difference between success and failure in its Third Initiation.

* * *

Woven through this book is the image of the owl, which came to me in visions of the Temple and the Mahanta's mission. As mentioned in a previous chapter, the ECK Master Milarepa told me in a dream that those ten owls were here on planet earth for an important mission. With my interest in owls, it was only natural for me to believe they have a strong connection to this global initiation.

The ECK Masters wanted the Temple of ECK because humanity needs to take a spiritual step forward, to move up to the Third Initiation. The outstanding quality which must be demonstrated at the Third Initiation is self-responsibility. And I believe the critical responsibility which humanity faces at this time in history is responsibility for the environment. For if we fail on that one, the planet will become unlivable.

Just as the Temple of ECK is the dividing line between the world's Second and Third initiation, for me the northern spotted owl has become a metaphor for the battle over the environment. This was brought home very clearly to me in my small hometown of Roseburg, Oregon.

I was living in Roseburg in 1989 when construction on the Temple of ECK was begun. At the time the controversy over the northern spotted owl was heating up in Oregon. And in my own personal life, I was going through a series of inner preparations for my next initiation in ECK.

Any time an individual receives an initiation in ECK, the whole world is lifted a little by it. In this way, each of us can make a difference in the progress toward the global Third Initiation. It becomes a process whereby the inner and outer worlds begin to merge and blend. For me waking dreams are among the patterns that accompany this blending process.

Though I moved away from Roseburg in September 1989, the interplay between the northern spotted owl and the world initiation continued to manifest itself to me. The most recent expression of this was a waking dream that began when I was in the middle of writing this book.

I was writing the chapter on the Holy Fire of ECK and had gotten to the point where I'd just described the dream vision of Milarepa and the ten owls. A phone call came from my mother. She was ill and had to go into the hospital for surgery, so she asked if I could come down to Roseburg and help out for a few days.

On the trip down, I felt there was a deeper significance to this visit than appeared on the surface. I arrived at my parents' home on Friday evening of May 15, 1992. That night, during contemplation, I asked the Mahanta to show me the deeper significance of the trip. It so happened that someone had left a book in the bedroom nightstand. Picking it up, I was intrigued to see the title: *Gifts of an Eagle.*

I closed my eyes, sang the sacred word *HU* a few times, and opened the book at random. Here is what I read: "The whole thing had to be carried out cautiously. He didn't want to endanger the owls."[2] This was the first strong hint of the owl theme that weekend.

The next morning came the second message. My father, who enjoys collecting used books and giving them to people, had one for me. "Here, son," he said, "I picked this up for twenty-five cents at a library sale." The book was one volume of an old children's encyclopedia. On the cover was a painting of a large white owl.

Shortly after breakfast, I took my mother to the hospital. As I walked by a newspaper box, a headline on a national newspaper caught my attention: "Owls lose 'God squad' vote." The "God squad" was a government panel, so called because it had been given power over the fate of endangered species.

What was the Mahanta telling me on this trip to Roseburg? I had to go to Roseburg because my mother was ill and needed help. On another level, Mother Earth was ill and needed help. This message was coming through to me in the repeated metaphor of the owls.

Another headline that dominated the news that weekend was in itself a related waking dream. The space shuttle *Endeavour* had been sent into space to rescue a newly launched communications satellite. The satellite had been mispositioned in space and was useless unless the shuttle astronauts could boost it into proper orbit.

The satellite would be one of many used to handle

TV broadcasts for the 1992 Summer Olympics. It took three space-walking astronauts to wrestle the cylinder-shaped satellite into place so it could be assisted into its proper orbit.

What was the waking dream in all of this?

Astronauts were trying to fix a communications satellite which would broadcast the world's oldest cooperative enterprise—the Olympics. It seemed to me that above the earth and down on the earth, the waking dream was crying out, We have a big problem here. We need to communicate, to cooperate, if we are to move forward spiritually.

Unlike an individual initiation, a global one doesn't happen in a day. Nine is primarily the number of initiation, and it is in this decade of the nineties that the global Third Initiation can occur. At least enough of it can occur to help the human race survive the tremendous challenges we face. The Temple of ECK is humanity's toehold on the cliff of a global initiation. It has opened the door for a greater flow of the Light and Sound of God into the world. It is up to us to seize the opportunity and make the most of it.

11

The Celestial Temple of ECK

The ECK can weave the most beautiful patterns on the fabric of time and space. They are there in the equations of the physicist, in the patterns of nature, and in the drama of human history. Beautiful they are, but also necessary. Many of them are the expressions of spiritual laws, such as the Law of Economy.

Innate in Soul is the urge to discover the ways of Divine Spirit. One of life's greatest pleasures is the delight that comes with a new insight into the way the ECK works. Whether the tickle of a sudden Aha! or the sublime ecstasy of a profound revelation, it is Divine Spirit moving through us. Which leads to the story of this chapter.

In August 1991 I decided it was time to take a vacation; I hadn't had one in two years. As a family we decided to take a trip around the scenic Olympic Peninsula of Washington State. Just before we departed on the morning of August 11, I was rearranging some furniture and found behind my desk the photo of Sri Harold's ground-breaking ceremony for the Temple of ECK. I was very happy to recover the photo, for it had disappeared months ago and I had searched everywhere trying to find it.

As I put the picture back on my desk, I got one of those tingly feelings that so often touch me when the Mahanta is trying to tell me something. There is a message in the finding of this photo just as we are leaving on this vacation, I thought. During the coming journey the ECK may well be giving me another insight on the Temple of ECK.

As so often happened before, significant insights given me by the Mahanta about his mission occurred at the same time as dramatic world events. During the vacation trip, there was a coup attempt in the Soviet Union. A group of communist hard-liners seized power from President Gorbachev, put him under house arrest, and made a last-ditch effort to keep control over the Soviet empire. It was the move everyone feared.

In the ensuing chaos, a popular revolt combined with the disorganization of the plotters enabled the coup to be reversed. But it spelled the end of the Soviet Union and Gorbachev's efforts to hold it together.

My vacation became a strange contrast of listening to the alarming news reports on the one hand and relaxing in the tranquil beauty of the Olympic Peninsula on the other. Between these two extremes, new insights on the Temple of ECK came to me.

On the north side of the peninsula we stopped to swim and relax at a deep, clear lake called Crescent Lake. While playing along the beach, my older daughter found a remarkable stone. It was perfectly round, uniformly flat, and pure white, about the size of a silver dollar. I examined the stone, wondering where it could have come from. The lakeshore where we were swimming was covered with thick, round stones which were dark gray or black.

I figured the white stone must have been brought from another region and thrown into the lake. But a few minutes later my daughter shouted, "Look, I found another one. And look, here's another!" I helped her look for more, and within a quarter of an hour we had found exactly seventeen white stones. They were all so identical in size, shape, and thickness that it was hard to tell them apart. Strangely, even though we continued looking for over an hour, we couldn't find one more white stone anywhere.

Soon we were all back in the car, driving on to another place to visit. As I drove along, I kept thinking about those seventeen white stones. The Mahanta, the Inner Master, gave me a little direction: "Think of this like a dream. How would you interpret this if it were a dream?" I thought it over for a while, but got nowhere with it.

"Where did you find the stones?" the Inner Master asked. "By Crescent Lake," I answered. "And what does the word *Crescent* suggest to you?" came the next leading question. "The crescent moon," I answered in my thoughts. "Now work with that idea," was the response.

So I pondered on that a little while. The round white stones seemed to me like little full moons. "Well," I ventured, "how about this? The seventeen white stones represent seventeen full moons, or a seventeen-month cycle. They are also like silver dollars, so they represent something of value." The Inner Master said, "You're getting warmer."

But that was as far as I could go with it. I couldn't come up with any great insights. I find that this is often the way the Mahanta works with us. He gives a clue, a thought, or an idea. By contemplating on it and working with it, we start to see it from many different angles.

131

No more thought was given to the stones until we got home from the vacation. Then one evening I was sitting at the kitchen table sipping a cup of tea and doodling with a paper and pencil. I sketched out a little picture of the Temple of ECK, with its main level and the ziggurat roof. Pretending my pencil was a little man walking up the ziggurat steps, I counted the steps: One, two, three, four, five, six, seven, eight, and nine at the top. Now let's go down the other side. Ten, eleven, twelve, thirteen, fourteen, fifteen, sixteen, seventeen.

Hmmm. If you go up to the top of the ziggurat and back down the other side, that's seventeen steps. And the seventeen white stones represent a seventeen-month cycle. Then it started to fit together. For me the Temple cycle began on May 22, 1989. It finished on October 22, 1990, at the dedication ceremony. That was a seventeen-month cycle.

The *spatial* architecture of the Temple ziggurat was reflected in the *time* of its cycle of manifestation. As Sri Harold writes in *The Temple of ECK:* "A pale golden ziggurat crowns the Temple. The stepped, pyramidal roof is reminiscent of architecture common to ancient Sumer, Babylonia, and Assyria. The design symbolizes mankind's spiritual journey up the plateaus of life. Humanity starts at the level of human consciousness and makes its deliberate way to the summit, which is God Consciousness."[1]

But the ascent up the spiritual mountain is only half the journey. The illuminated Soul must now come back down the mountain and share Its light with others. In telling his story of God-Realization in *Child in the Wilderness,* Sri Harold writes: "It starts at the bottom, on a plain—as a regular story might—and goes to the top of the hill. But instead of ending there with God-

Realization, as one might expect, the storyline continues down the hill until it again reaches the plain of everyday living on the other side."[2]

So the seventeen white stones and the seventeen-month Temple cycle had led me to an image of the full process of going to the top of the spiritual mountain and coming back down again.

After this became clear to me, my thoughts went back to the cycle I wrote about in chapter 8. That was the cycle where the whole solar system comes into a gravitational balance around the sun and which happens only a few times every thousand years. One particular cycle ran from April 28, 1989, to December 23, 1990. In other words it began just before the seventeen-month Temple cycle and ended just after it.

I see this cycle as the celestial correspondence in time of the physical Temple. Over the next few days the ECK led me to one insight after another on this celestial aspect of the Temple of ECK. I was shown a grand picture of interlocking cycles. These cycles ranged from a month up to 3,600 years. The whole structure was keyed to the number nine, expressive of the Mahanta's mission in this age.

Some investigators of the great pyramid of Khufu at Giza claim to have found in its measurements thousands of years of prophecy. I was shown how the Temple of ECK has its own prophecies built into it. And this brings out an interesting point. The Temple architects and builders were all vehicles for this expression in time and space of these divine mysteries.

On the practical level the people who worked on the Temple were just trying to meet deadlines, beat the weather, and construct a good building. But through it all, I feel they were moving in harmony with the dance of the cosmos, with tides of cycles lasting thousands of years, with the ageless mission of the Mahanta.

I have seen many functions for the Temple of ECK. Some of them are: (1) as a link between humanity and God, (2) as a channel for Divine Spirit, or ECK, to flow into the world, (3) as an altar for that eternal flame called the Holy Fire of ECK, and (4) as an embodiment in stone of certain proportions which express cosmic cycles and prophecies concerning the spiritual unfoldment of the human race.

These functions fit in perfectly with the ziggurat roof that Sri Harold chose for the Temple. The following statements by scholar Zecharia Sitchin about ancient Middle-Eastern ziggurat temples may illuminate the Temple of ECK's spiritual purpose:

> The Akkadian/Babylonian name for these structures, *zukiratu,* connoted "tube of divine spirit." The Sumerians called the ziggurats ESH; the term denoted "supreme" or "most high"—as indeed these structures were. It could also denote a numerical entity relating to the "measuring" aspect of the ziggurats. And it also meant "a heat source" ("fire" in Akkadian and Hebrew).[3]

The author of the above quote also references the following statement by the scholar Samuel N. Kramer:

> The ziggurat, the stagetower, which became the hallmark of Mesopotamian temple architecture . . . was intended to serve as a connecting link, both real and symbolic, between the gods in heaven and the mortals on earth.[4]

In October 1991 I journeyed to the ECK Worldwide Seminar in Minneapolis, Minnesota. During this trip I visited the Temple of ECK for the first time. After a tour of the Temple, I joined three friends for a walk along Lake Ann, which borders the Temple grounds.

There I distributed the seventeen white stones among us, and we took turns skipping them out on the lake. It was a magical moment for me, my token of appreciation to the Mahanta for the insights he'd given me on the significance of the Temple.

* * *

The prophecies and cycles that I believe are built into the Temple of ECK are not just curiosities with no practical consequence. I would like to give one instance of what I mean.

In September 1990 the ECKists here in Portland, Oregon, decided to try to find a new ECKANKAR Center. We searched but couldn't find anything to match our needs and budget. So we decided to extend the lease on our current ECK Center and try again later. Into early 1992 the search continued. Finally an excellent building was found with adequate room for growth. We moved to the new ECK Center on March 29, 1992.

While this effort to move to a new ECK Center was going on, some parallel home-hunting was occurring in my own life. My family had been searching for a house to buy for over eight months. No matter how hard we tried or how many houses we looked at, nothing worked out. That is, until March 1992. The same day the Portland ECKANKAR group signed the lease on the new ECK Center, my wife and I closed on our new house. We even moved to our new house on March 29, the same day as the move to the new ECK Center.

A third move was also pending. The company I work for had been trying to move my department of several hundred people across town to a new building. There were endless meetings, promises, and excuses. One problem after another arose, blocking the move. Finally, at the same time the ECK Center moved and my family moved, my department at work moved.

I asked the Mahanta why all of these moves were blocked until the magic date of late March, 1992. That night in a dream I was shown a different view of the seventeen-month cycle I had discovered earlier. The seventeen-month cycle that ran from May 22, 1989, to October 22, 1990, was the upswing of a cycle. A seventeen-month downswing had run from October 22, 1990, through March 22, 1992. On March 22 the cycle was on the upswing again, flowing out in a new wave of uplifting energy. It was at that time that all of the obstacles broke loose and everyone was able to move.

Please don't conclude from this example that you should plan anything according to this cycle. The ECK will let each of us know the right time and place to do Its work. For certain inner reasons, the Portland ECKANKAR group was attuned to this particular cycle. This attunement was dramatized for us a little later.

In a Higher Initiate's meeting on February 9, 1992, at the old ECKANKAR Center it was suggested we have a dedication ceremony for the new ECK Center. We wanted to model it after the dedication ceremony which was held at the Temple of ECK in 1990. Another suggestion was to create a mission statement for the new center. We wanted the new center to be a conscious extension of the Temple of ECK and the Mahanta's mission.

I volunteered to draft a mission statement. This mission statement was drawn from points Sri Harold had made in his article in the *Mystic World* titled "The ECK Temple: A Gift to the World." The final version of our mission statement was finished on April 9 and contained nine mission statements. Only after it was finished did I notice how this project was attuned to the number nine—from its inception on February 9 to its completion on April 9 to its nine statements.

I felt this was because we were trying to align ourselves with the Mahanta's mission to lift ECKANKAR to Consciousness Nine. The other Higher Initiates in the area approved the final draft, and it was ready to be read at the dedication ceremony. Then a very interesting thing happened.

It was during the time of the 1992 ECK Spring-time Seminar in Washington, D.C. I had not been able to go. On Monday evening I sat down to contemplate. Usually, I just sit, sing HU, and see what comes. But that evening I felt I should contemplate on the Mahanta's mission. About five minutes into the contemplation, the phone rang. I really didn't want to get up and answer it. But I figured if the phone rang at that moment, I should try to make the most of it.

As I got up and walked to the phone, I said to myself, No matter who is on that phone, I'm going to imagine it is the Mahanta calling. And no matter what they say, I'm going to imagine it is a message on the Mahanta's mission.

It was a fellow Higher Initiate from Portland, and he was calling from Washington, D.C., where he'd been attending the Springtime Seminar. In fact, this was the person who had originally suggested we have a dedication ceremony for our new ECK Center.

The caller explained that that weekend Sri Harold had issued a mission statement for ECKANKAR! He thought we ought to incorporate it into the mission statement we'd composed for the new ECKANKAR Center. After some discussion and consultation with the other Higher Initiates, we felt we should just discard our own mission statement and use the Mahanta's. We had been on the right track in trying to come up with a mission statement. But the Mahanta, in his wisdom, was able to say in one sentence what we'd been trying to say in nine!

This whole episode was a real lesson. I felt that the Mahanta was doing two things. First, he was confirming for us that our plans were inspired by the ECK. Second, he was demonstrating divine simplicity. Here is the essence of Sri Harold's mission statement for ECKANKAR:

"The mission of ECKANKAR is to show an individual the way home to God."

* * *

You may wish to try the following contemplation. In the quote below, Paul Twitchell lists the nine steps on the ladder of God. Choose a step that matches your level of initiation or seems right to you at this time. First, read what Paul has written for that particular step. It will be your contemplation seed.

Next, imagine yourself standing or sitting in the Soul body on that step of the ziggurat of the Temple of ECK. While there, contemplate on the quote for that step. Here is Paul's quote from *The ECK-Vidya, Ancient Science of Prophecy:*

> Nine steps on the ladder is a symbolism of the nine steps or stages of the spiritual development of an ECKist, toward becoming a co-worker with God. . . . They are: (1) The stage of joy, in which you, the ECKist, develop your holy nature and discard wrong views. (2) The stage of Illumination, in which you attain perfection of patience or humility, and also the deepest introspective insight. (3) The stage of divine knowledge in which you achieve and realize the harmony of worldly truth and supreme truth. (4) The stage of perfec-

tion in which you receive the divine wisdom as your own. (5) The stage of perfection in which you receive the ability to save all beings. (6) The stage of perfection in which you realize that all things are false except the God nature of all creatures and things. (7) The stage in which you attain the ten holy powers and can create miracles with humility. (8) The stage of mastery of perfect realization in which you can preach the law to save all creatures. (9) The stage of perfection in which you can be supreme in all things, to create the higher miracles without the knowledge of people, accept karma and be with the Living ECK Master to help in his work."[5]

12

The Universal Body
of the Mahanta

The ECK Masters have been key agents in the inspiration and unfoldment of all civilizations. One Master's mission builds on another's, carrying the plan of the spiritual hierarchy another step further.

Often the ECK Masters are like secret agents, working quietly behind the scenes as they serve the ECK. On the occasions when their missions are made public, the student of ECK has an opportunity to study the effects of these Masters' missions on the world.

This chapter traces the growth of an idea planted by two well-known ECK Masters of classical Greece. It is an idea which has evolved through the centuries, and I feel it may have importance for the current mission of ECKANKAR in this world.

The ancient Greek city-states achieved an astonishing richness and variety in their cultures. They burst forth upon western civilization with a zest for the creative life. Their talented achievements were so rich and diverse, they would become the measure of culture for fifteen centuries. In all history no culture has so passionately adored another culture as the West has adored the Greeks.

141

I feel this golden age of Greece was due in great part to the work of a number of ECK Masters. The two who concern us in this chapter are Phidias and Pythagoras. Both had a strong influence on the culture of the sixth and fifth centuries B.C. Phidias primarily inspired the arts, and Pythagoras the sciences. But at that time, as in any golden age, there was not the split between the arts and sciences which emerged later in history.

As I see it, there was one key seed which both of these ECK Masters had a hand in nurturing, each in their own field of service. It was the idea of a divine proportion, a standard of measure which worked equally well in the arts and the sciences.

Phidias used this proportion in his design of that most classic of all ancient temples, the Parthenon on the Acropolis in Athens. And Pythagoras extolled the wonders of the same proportion to his students. What does such an idea have to do with the universal body of the Mahanta? The answer to that question leads to one of the most fascinating golden threads of history.

The story begins with Pythagoras. He was for a while a resident of the island of Samos. But disliking the government, he left the island and traveled abroad. Tradition says he visited Egypt and gathered much of his wisdom in that country.

Ultimately he settled in a Greek city in southern Italy called Crotone. There Pythagoras founded a society of disciples, open equally to men and women. Property was held in common, and there was a communal life.[1]

Bertrand Russell wrote in his *History of Western Philosophy:* "Pythagoras . . . was intellectually one of the most important men that ever lived"[2] and "one of the most interesting and puzzling men in history."[3]

142

Also, "I do not know of any other man who has been as influential as he was in the sphere of thought. . . . The whole conception of an eternal world, revealed to the intellect but not to the senses, is derived from him. But for him, Christians would not have thought of Christ as the Word."[4]

Pythagoras had a special passion for mathematics. He saw numbers as the ordering principle of creation and discovered the mathematical foundations of music. But one of the discoveries which he held in highest regard was the ratio which Kepler later called "the divine proportion." This ratio, which is approximately equal to 8:5 or 1.6, is most perfectly expressed in the five-pointed star (see illustration).

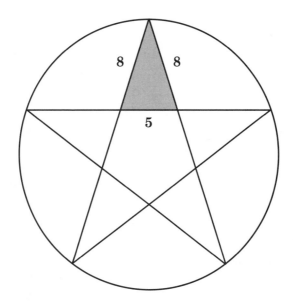

The divine proportion in the pentacle. The sides and base of each point of the star are equal to this proportion, or about 8:5.

The pentacle, or five-pointed star, became the symbol of the Pythagorean brotherhood and was thought to convey health.[5]

Why was Pythagoras so intrigued by this proportion? There were two key reasons.

First, the divine proportion was found to be a "golden mean." This is the mean between two parts such that the lesser part is to the greater as the greater part is to the whole. In other words, it is the bridge of harmony between the microcosm and the macrocosm.

The second reason arises from the study of solid geometry. The school of Pythagoras knew there were only five regular convex solids, each of which could be circumscribed by a sphere. Of these five the dodecahedron was held in special regard. Its twelve faces were pentagons, which like five-pointed stars, express the divine proportion. And the ratio of the radius of the solid's circumcircle to any side was also the same proportion. To the Pythagoreans, the dodecahedron was a symbol of the universe, its twelve faces corresponding to the twelve signs of the zodiac.[6]

Paul Twitchell writes, "The number twelve has profound significance in many areas of ECKANKAR, the Ancient Science of Soul Travel. It has been said that all human life, as well as the spiritual is attuned to this number."[7] Pythagoras knew this too and used the twelve-sided solid, and the divine proportion, as keys to the spiritual mysteries.

A few years after Pythagoras came the ECK Master Phidias. He lived and worked in Athens and was considered the finest of the Greek sculptors.[8] Phidias worked on the Parthenon, the single most famous and admired Greek building. It was erected on the Acropolis in Athens between 447 and 432 B.C. and dedicated to the city's patron goddess, Athena

144

Parthenos (the virgin Athena).[9]

Paul Twitchell writes of Phidias, "He tried to put into this temple his ideal of the ECK, and one who is fortunate enough to see and study the Parthenon will find the ancient mysteries of ECK."[10]

I believe "the ancient mysteries of ECK" which Paul is referring to include the divine proportion. Author Gyorgi Doczi refers to the Parthenon and the golden proportion in his amazing book *The Power of Limits*. In it he shows how the Parthenon is built upon layer after layer of divine proportion, with the front of the edifice fitting into a rectangle of divine proportion.[11]

H.E. Huntley, in his book *The Divine Proportion*, mentions that Phidias, the famous Greek sculptor, made use of the divine proportion in the Parthenon. Huntley goes on to say, it was suggested in the early days of the present century that the Greek letter ϕ — the initial letter of Phidias's name — should be adopted to designate the golden ratio.[12] And today phi (ϕ) is still used to designate the divine proportion.

So Phidias helped introduce the mysteries of the divine proportion into western civilization, and twenty-five centuries later it is still referred to by the first Greek letter of his name!

Pythagoras and Phidias had planted the seed of an important spiritual principle in the sixth and fifth centuries B.C. But that was only a beginning. The Greeks were able to realize the beauty of the divine proportion in mathematics and architecture but didn't take the concept any further that we know of. The golden age of Greece faded into history and was almost totally forgotten in the dark age that followed.

*   *   *

The golden mean, or divine proportion, was largely ignored until the Italian Renaissance. At that time, as western civilization began to burst forth into another creative cycle, the divine proportion came back into fashion again.

This wasn't a coincidence. Golden ages emerge when there is a good relation between the physical and spiritual worlds, between the microcosm and the macrocosm. And the divine proportion is an expression of this. As the ECK Master Rebazar Tarzs tells Paul Twitchell in a discourse on aesthetics, "Culture, literature, art, do not make civilization. Refined tastes do not make civilization. . . . Wisdom, power and freedom make civilization and these three are the essence of pure spirit. Spirituality is always abundant in every Golden Age.

"This is what makes it golden!"[13]

As the Renaissance thinkers turned the spotlight of their research on the divine proportion, they discovered a whole new dimension of it. The human body, from head to toe, is a symphony of divine proportion. In *The Power of Limits,* Doczi shows this by using Leonardo DaVinci's famous drawing, *Canon of Proportion.* In that drawing are seventeen examples of the divine proportion in the human frame.[14]

This discovery held a key new insight. It showed that the human body itself was built on the same mysterious proportion as the pentacle. Not only temples like the Parthenon, but the temple of the human Soul, were constructed along the lines of the divine proportion.

As western culture moved out of the Renaissance, it turned toward a materialism that was as one-sided as the mysticism of the Middle Ages. Again the unity of art, science, and religion was split apart. And the divine proportion, which was a key thread that held them all together, fell out of fashion.

*   *   *

In the last decades of the twentieth century, it seems to me that the human race is once again returning to a balance between its spiritual and material concerns. And once again I see this signaled by the emergence of a new golden age and a rebirth in popularity of the divine proportion.

As this cycle returns again on a higher plane, it seems the ECK Masters are finally ready to harvest the fruit of the seed planted over two millennia ago by Pythagoras and Phidias. For I believe the real and spiritual significance of the divine proportion is now being realized. And what is this significance? That the divine proportion can be a bridge between the microcosm of the individual and the macrocosm of his spiritual community.

Gyorgi Doczi gets very close to the ECK viewpoint when he writes, "The power of the golden section [i.e., the divine proportion] to create harmony arises from its unique capacity to unite the different parts of a whole so that each preserves its own identity, and yet blends into the greater pattern of a single whole."[15] And "We complement our own and others' shortcomings, creating thereby living harmony in the art of life, comparable to the harmonies created in music, dance, marble, wood and clay. It is possible to live in this way because the proportions of reciprocal sharing, nature's own golden proportions, are built into our own nature, into our bodies and minds."[16]

Doczi has found the bridge that spans the microcosm and the macrocosm—the harmonious spiritual community, each part working for the good of the whole. But it remained for the building of the Temple of ECK for a fuller realization of the spiritual meaning of the divine proportion.

ECKist David Calvo, in a truly inspired article,

found the key. Building on Leonardo Da Vinci's *Canon of Proportion* (mentioned above), Calvo showed how the human form can be superimposed over the Temple of ECK. He believes the Temple is a macrocosmic body, composed of all those who love and serve through the ECK. In other words, it is a doorway into the body of Divine Spirit, the universal body of the Mahanta. He writes:

> Is it then possible that we can become the *Spirit of ECKANKAR,* our journey being into the heart of God? . . . I hope so, because *what we are witnessing* is the flight from self to selflessness, from the microcosmic world *across the dotted line* to the worlds of the macrocosm, the universal body of God.[17]

Many of the great temples of the world exhibit the divine proportion. Doczi gives numerous examples, including Stonehenge, the Great Pyramid of Egypt, the Parthenon, the Ziggurats of Mesopotamia, and others.[18] Either consciously or intuitively, architects have built this spiritual key into their masterpieces.

Why? The real temple of Divine Spirit is the human body. It is a form built upon the divine proportion. When an architect designs a temple, he is building a macrocosmic body of the spiritual community. I believe that if he is a channel for Divine Spirit, his work will embody in some way a motif which creates a harmonious blending of the individual members who compose the community. To me, this is the highest calling of architecture.

The ECK Masters gave the awareness of the divine proportion to the human race for just this purpose. That this proportion has been much admired during the various golden ages of civilization is a testament to its effectiveness. However, with the Temple of ECK

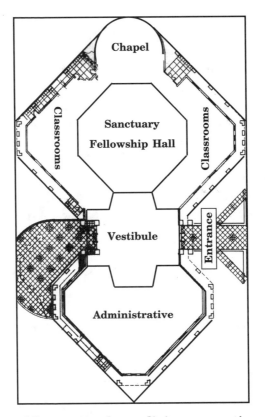

The golden rectangle, or divine proportion, around the Temple of ECK. The doorway into the universal body of the Mahanta.

it has the potential to reach its most divine expression.

In the above illustration I have shown an aerial-view outline of the Temple of ECK, with a rectangle of divine proportion drawn around it. I see it as a giant door, signifying that the Temple is a spiritual doorway between the worlds of Divine Spirit and the earth world. Notice how the top line of the rectangle touches the chapel portion of the Temple. David Calvo in his article saw the center of the chapel as the Third Eye, or Spiritual Eye, in the body of the Temple.

In the chapter titled "Field of Dreams" I discussed

a dream in which Sri Harold showed me a baseball diamond where the Temple of ECK was being built. He led me to second base and told me, "This will be the exact entrance to the Temple of ECK." At the time, the dream made no sense. It was only after David Calvo's article came out that the answer to the dream was given me. The Mahanta had shown me, in my own way, the same thing he had shown David.

In the next illustration I have shown a pair of David's sketches. Around the larger one, I have drawn a baseball diamond. Second base of the baseball diamond sits exactly at the top of the Temple, above where David located the Third Eye of the macrocosmic man. The Third Eye is located in the human body between the eyebrows at the base of the forehead. It is the doorway into the worlds of Divine Spirit. Soul

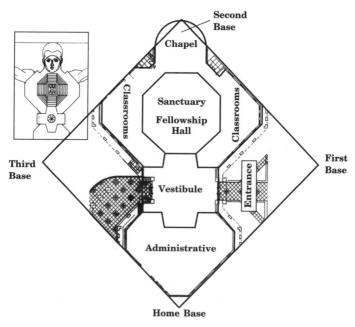

Field of Dreams

often enters and exits the physical body through this door.

Yet by telling me second base was the exact entrance into the Temple, Sri Harold was revealing that this was the Third Eye of the Temple of ECK. The *physical* entrance to the Temple is in the vestibule. But I believe the chapel serves as a *spiritual* entrance. This agrees with David Calvo's vision of the Temple, in which he found the Third Eye of the Temple in the chapel.

* * *

The preceding has laid the groundwork for this chapter's title, "The Universal Body of the Mahanta." What does this expression mean? Book Two of *The Shariyat-Ki-Sugmad* explains:

> Those who follow the ECK believe that it is when they are completely what the SUGMAD wants them to be that they can contribute most to the total life of the body of the Mahanta, the Living ECK Master of which they are a member, and to the life of the whole human race to which they belong; a belief based on their whole understanding of the spiritual works of ECK as the body of the Mahanta, and of the whole world as created by the SUGMAD. Therefore, it functions properly only when every part of it is in complete obedience to God.[19]

I believe the above quote states the mission of all ECKists and of the Temple of ECK: service to the SUGMAD; the Mahanta, the Living ECK Master; and to the whole world. Sri Harold has said a number of times that his mission is to bring the teachings of ECK to the whole world. The Temple of ECK is the bridge that will make this mission possible.

As Calvo explained in his article on the Temple as

macrocosmic body, it is we, the ECK community around the world, who complete the form. We are the arms and legs, the feet and hands, that walk the earth and reach out to serve.

In a similar way, the divine proportion is more implicit than explicit in the Temple of ECK. It is there in the microcosmic human form, extended out into the body of ECK servers, "creating thereby living harmony in the art of life" to re-quote Doczi. This idea will be developed more in a moment, later in the chapter.

The Shariyat continues on the theme with these words: "If the doctrine of the body of the Mahanta as the spirit in and of the ECK is taken seriously, and due significance given to the variety of tasks within the body of the Mahanta, then the ECKist's life can be seen as one of those tasks, complementing others and complemented by them."[20]

Each of us dwells in our little temple, our human body. Collectively we dwell in the universal body of the Mahanta. The ECK Master Lai Tsi states it this way, "It is the ECK which envelopes all bodies of man within Itself."[21]

How does one enter into the body of the Mahanta? In one sense, we are all in it right now, for we live and move and have our being within the ECK. But to become a *conscious* member requires the spiritual initiation. *The Shariyat* says, "Indeed, the whole thesis of the ECK chela's life is that he does in his own peculiar way what all ECKists are called upon to do; that their vows are a specific way of carrying out the initiation promises and that their community life is a particular manifestation of the life of the ECK, the body of the Mahanta of which they were made a member at the initiation of the First Circle."[22]

There is a vast difference between being an unconscious part of this body and being a conscious part. The many initiations in ECK are a progressive realization of just what the universal body of the Mahanta is. *The Shariyat* says, "The inner secret of the body can be made known only by the Mahanta, and he is the only one empowered by the SUGMAD to reveal it."[23]

Just as the body has its inner secret, so too does that body called the Temple of ECK. It exists on many levels, and its full impact on the destiny of the human race lies hidden in the heart of the ECK.

*   *   *

We saw in the beginning of this chapter how the divine proportion is expressed in the pentacle, or five-pointed star. The human body, also based on the divine proportion, can be symbolized by the pentacle. As Paul Twitchell writes in *The ECK Vidya, Ancient Science of Prophecy:*

> Man himself is this pentacle, for with his hands out-stretched, his feet spread and his head erect, he forms the 5-pointed star.
>
> The flames, which are said to issue from the 5 points of the pentacle on the end of the wand are the powers inherent in the perfected body, the glorious robe of man's strength.[24]

This is the Holy Fire of ECK which dwells in the temple of the human body and in the Temple of ECK. To me, the five-pointed star represents the Temple, the house wherein dwells the Holy Spirit.

But Divine Spirit Itself, the ECK, is often symbolized by a six-pointed star. This is the Star of ECK, the Blue Star of the Mahanta. In the little temple of the human body, the Blue Star hovers at the Spiritual Eye, waiting to guide Soul home to God. In the Temple of ECK, the six-pointed Blue Star hovers over the sanctuary, a constant reminder of Divine Spirit. When the bodily temple is illuminated by Spirit, it becomes a miniature Temple of Golden Wisdom.

I believe the number eleven signifies the union of Spirit (the six-pointed star) and Its Temple (the five-pointed star), whether that temple be the human body or a stone edifice.

The Temple of ECK is the fifth major Temple of Golden Wisdom on the physical plane. Sri Harold has said: "The other four exist on a supra-physical level, meaning they are only visible through the Spiritual Eye."[25] The three others on earth are the Faqiti Monastery in the Gobi Desert, the Katsupari Monastery in Tibet, and the Gare Hira Temple of Golden Wisdom at the spiritual city of Agam Des. The fourth is the House of Moksha in the city of Retz, on Venus.

The building of the Temple of ECK at Chanhassen completes a symbolic five-pointed star of Golden Wisdom Temples on the physical plane. All together they form what might be called a cosmic Temple of Temples. The divine proportion has now reached out into the solar system, linking Earth and Venus in a great five-pointed star.

This is more than a poetic idea. There is an amazing relationship that exists astronomically between Earth and Venus. It takes Earth 365 days to orbit the sun. It takes Venus 225 days. But the ratio of these two orbital periods is very close to the Divine Proportion, or about 8:5. Due to the laws of celestial mechanics there is a very striking consequence of this fact.

Earth and Venus have a conjunction pattern that occurs five times every eight years. From the point of view of Earth, these five conjunctions form the points of a five-pointed star. Researcher Neil Michelsen made a computer-generated graph of the orbital dance between Venus and Earth. He shows the result on page 233 of his book *Tables of Planetary Phenomena*. It is a pentacle in the form of a lovely five-petaled flower.

For me, a five-pointed star traced in space between these five points signifies the Light of ECK. And I also believe the Sound is there as well.

I believe that if one were to observe our solar system from a great distance, one would be able to perceive vibrations based on the orbital periods of the planets as they orbit the sun. Since the ratio of the orbital periods of Venus and Earth approximates the divine proportion, if the vibrations of these two planets were to be perceived in an atmosphere, they would combine to form a musical chord, a major sixth—the divine proportion.

H.E. Huntley, in his book *The Divine Proportion,* has some very illuminating comments on the major-sixth interval. He quotes studies which have been done in aesthetics which show that people find most pleasing those musical intervals which are most consonant. The three which are most pleasing to the ear are the unison, the octave, and the major sixth. Based on the ratio of its frequencies, the major sixth is the divine proportion as it manifests in sound and was found for most people to be pleasing to the ear above all others.[26]

Since the divine proportion brings harmony, or consonance, and relates the microcosm to the macrocosm, it is not surprising that it is as pleasing in sound as it is in form.

I don't know if these astronomical harmonies were a factor in the Vairagi ECK Masters' choice of Earth and Venus as the planets in our system upon which to build their temples. In any case, the divine proportion extends itself far into space, linking us into the community of planets. Or as *The Shariyat-Ki-Sugmad,* Book Two, says, "The community of ECK is international, interplanetary, interpsychic, and interspiritual."[27]

* * *

You may wish to use the following spiritual exercise, which works well alone or in a group.

Envision before you the universal body of the Mahanta, in whatever form it appears to you. See how it is made up of all the initiates in ECK—a living, breathing community.

Now move forward and merge into the body of the Mahanta. Find your place within it. Where are you? How is your current mission, or life focus, related to your place in the universal body?

Now, as you sing HU, imagine the universal body singing HU and feel how it is a powerful conduit for God's love. See and feel how every part of the body has its importance and serves the whole. Notice how all the parts complement each other.

Move around within the body, if you wish, and see how it feels to serve in different areas. Contemplate on how the body of ECK initiates relates to the whole body of the ECK.

Epilogue: The Visitation

It was September 8, 1991. The next day would mark the anniversary of my dramatic Consciousness-Nine vision. I took my children to the neighborhood playground for an hour of fun. As I watched them on the merry-go-round, my thoughts turned back to the vision and the promise it held for ECKANKAR and the world. I wondered about the Nine Silent Ones, those mysterious ECK Masters who guide the world's destiny, and what part they played in this historic event.

My train of thought was suddenly interrupted by the approach of a flock of seagulls. They came winging in from the north in single file, descending toward us as they came closer. When they reached us at the merry-go-round, they formed themselves into a circle about twenty feet over our heads. Around and around they flew in a tight circle. They made not a sound, except for the soft swishing of air over their wings.

As they kept swirling round and round, I wondered what they were looking for. We had no food to attract them. And they weren't making the usual noisy seagull conversation among themselves. I counted them, and there were nine. The magic of their dance began to touch me, and I just smiled and waved at them. Then, abruptly they broke their circle and headed back to the north in single file.

Later that night I sat down at my computer to write about the experience. At the end of the description, I wrote this: "Who knows? Perhaps they were the Nine Silent Ones." The moment I put the period on that last sentence, the power went out in my house. Looking out the window, I saw the power was out in the whole neighborhood. Later I learned that it had gone out over much of the city. The hour was midnight, and the day 9-9-91 was being born at that moment.

Perhaps this was a visit of the Nine Silent Ones. Or maybe those were just nine seagulls acting under the inspiration of the ECK. But this I know—it was the Dream Weaver's promise: Consciousness Nine is being born in ECKANKAR. We can thank Sri Harold Klemp, the Mahanta, the Living ECK Master for this miracle.

Glossary

Words set in SMALL CAPS are defined elsewhere in the glossary.

ARAHATA. An experienced and qualified teacher for ECKANKAR classes.

CHELA. A spiritual student.

ECK. The Life Force, the Holy Spirit, or Audible Life Current which sustains all life.

ECKANKAR. Religion of the Light and Sound of God. Also known as the Ancient Science of SOUL TRAVEL. A truly spiritual religion for the individual in modern times, known as the secret path to God via dreams and SOUL TRAVEL. The teachings provide a framework for anyone to explore their own spiritual experiences. Established by Paul Twitchell, the modern-day founder, in 1965.

ECK MASTERS. Spiritual Masters who can assist and protect people in their spiritual studies and travels. The ECK Masters are from a long line of God-Realized SOULS who know the responsibility that goes with spiritual freedom.

HU. The secret name for God. The singing of the word HU, pronounced like the word *hue,* is considered a love song to God. It is sung in the ECK Worship Service.

INITIATION. Earned by the ECK member through spiritual unfoldment and service to God. The initiation is a private ceremony in which the individual is linked to the Sound and Light of God.

LIVING ECK MASTER. The title of the spiritual leader of ECKANKAR. His duty is to lead SOULS back to God. The Living ECK Master can assist spiritual students physically as the

Outer Master, in the dream state as the Dream Master, and in the spiritual worlds as the Inner Master. Sri Harold Klemp became the Living ECK Master in 1981.

MAHANTA. A title to describe the highest state of God Consciousness on earth, often embodied in the LIVING ECK MASTER. He is the Living Word.

PLANES. The levels of heaven, such as the Astral, Causal, Mental, Etheric, and Soul planes.

SATSANG. A class in which students of ECK study a monthly lesson from ECKANKAR.

THE SHARIYAT-KI-SUGMAD. The sacred scriptures of ECKANKAR. The scriptures are comprised of twelve volumes in the spiritual worlds. The first two were transcribed from the inner PLANES by Paul Twitchell, modern-day founder of ECKANKAR.

SOUL. The True Self. The inner, most sacred part of each person. Soul exists before birth and lives on after the death of the physical body. As a spark of God, Soul can see, know, and perceive all things. It is the creative center of Its own world.

SOUL TRAVEL. The expansion of consciousness. The ability of SOUL to transcend the physical body and travel into the spiritual worlds of God. Soul Travel is taught only by the LIVING ECK MASTER. It helps people unfold spiritually and can provide proof of the existence of God and life after death.

SOUND AND LIGHT OF ECK. The Holy Spirit. The two aspects through which God appears in the lower worlds. People can experience them by looking and listening within themselves and through SOUL TRAVEL.

SPIRITUAL EXERCISES OF ECK. The daily practice of certain techniques to get us in touch with the Light and Sound of God.

SUGMAD. A sacred name for God. SUGMAD is neither masculine nor feminine; IT is the source of all life.

WAH Z. The spiritual name of Sri Harold Klemp. It means the Secret Doctrine. It is his name in the spiritual worlds.

Notes

Chapter 1. A Prophecy Three Times Told

1. Harold Klemp, *Soul Travelers of the Far Country* (Minneapolis: ECKANKAR, 1987).

2. Ibid.

3. Harold Klemp, *Wisdom of the Heart* (Minneapolis: ECKANKAR, 1992).

4. Harold Klemp, *Soul Travelers of the Far Country* (Minneapolis: ECKANKAR, 1987).

Chapter 2. A Vision of the Mahanta's Mission

1. Harold Klemp, *Journey of Soul,* Mahanta Transcripts, Book One (Minneapolis: ECKANKAR, 1988).

2. Harold Klemp, *The Temple of ECK,* (Minneapolis: ECKANKAR, 1991).

3. *The Mystic World,* Spring 1988.

4. Ibid.

5. Harold Klemp, *Soul Travelers of the Far Country* (Minneapolis: ECKANKAR, 1987).

6. Harold Klemp, *The Living Word* (Minneapolis: ECKANKAR, 1989).

7. Harold Klemp, *Soul Travelers of the Far Country* (Minneapolis: ECKANKAR,1987).

8. Ibid.

9. Ibid.

10. Harold Klemp, *The Living Word* (Minneapolis: ECKANKAR, 1989).

11. Elisabeth Kübler-Ross, M.D., *On Death and Dying* (New York: Macmillan Publishing Co., Inc, 1969)

12. Harold Klemp, *The Living Word* (Minneapolis: ECKANKAR, 1989).

13. Ibid.

14. Harold Klemp, *The Holy Fire of ECK* (Minneapolis: ECKANKAR, 1993).

15. Ibid.

16. Harold Klemp, *The Living Word* (Minneapolis: ECKANKAR, 1989).

17. Ibid.

18. *The Mystic World,* Spring 1988.

19. *The Mystic World,* Spring 1985.

20. Harold Klemp, *Cloak of Consciousness,* Mahanta Transcripts, Book 5 (Minneapolis: ECKANKAR, 1991).

21. *The Mystic World,* Spring 1988.

22. Harold Klemp, *The Living Word* (Minneapolis: ECKANKAR, 1989).

23. *The Mystic World,* Spring 1988.

24. Harold Klemp, *Wisdom of the Heart* (Minneapolis: ECKANKAR, 1992).

25. Harold Klemp, *The Holy Fire of ECK* (Minneapolis: ECKANKAR, 1993).

26. Harold Klemp, *Wisdom of the Heart* (Minneapolis: ECKANKAR, 1992).

27. Harold Klemp, *The Holy Fire of ECK* (Minneapolis: ECKANKAR, 1993).

28. Ibid.

29. Ibid.

30. *The Mystic World,* Spring 1988.

31. Harold Klemp, *Wisdom of the Heart* (Minneapolis: ECKANKAR, 1992).

Chapter 3. Vision Quest One: On Sacred Ground

1. Medicine Hawk and Grey Cat, *American Indian Ceremonies, A Practical Workbook and Study Guide to the Medicine Path* (Petaluma: Inner Light Publications, 1990).

Chapter 4. The Bridge of Purification

1. Harold Klemp, *The Eternal Dreamer,* Mahanta Transcripts, Book 7 (Minneapolis: ECKANKAR, 1992).

2. Leslie Dunkling and William Gosling, *The Facts on File Dictionary of First Names* (New York: Facts on File Publications, 1984).

3. Paul Twitchell, *Stranger by the River* (Minneapolis: ECKANKAR, 1970, 1987).

4. Ibid.

5. Ibid.

6. Harold Klemp, *Child in the Wilderness* (Minneapolis: ECKANKAR, 1989).

Chapter 5. The HU Heard round the World

1. John W. Wright, ed., *The Universal Almanac 1990* (Kansas City: Andrews and McMeel, 1990).

2. Harold Klemp, *The Temple of ECK* (Minneapolis: ECKANKAR, 1991).

3. *The Mystic World,* Winter 1989.

4. Paul Twitchell, "Leadership in ECK: Seat of Power" audiocassette (Minneapolis: ECKANKAR, 1979).

5. John W. Wright, ed., *The Universal Almanac 1990* (Kansas City: Andrews and McMeel, 1990).

6. Ray Grasse, "The Beijing Massacre: Death of the Piscean Age?" *Welcome to Planet Earth* (Volume 9, No. 2): 12.

7. Ibid.

8. John W. Wright, ed., *The Universal Almanac 1990* (Kansas City: Andrews and McMeel, 1990).

9. William R. Doerner, "Freedom Train." *Time* (October 16, 1989): 38–42.

10. Maxine Fields, *Baby Names from Around the World* (New York: Simon & Schuster Trade, 1990).

11. Leslie Dunkling and William Gosling, *The New American Dictionary of Baby Names* (New York: Signet, 1991).

12. Bob and Celeste Longacre, "Hurricanes: Spirit Winds of Change." *Welcome to Planet Earth* (Volume 9, No. 5): 15.

13. Ibid.

14. "Honecker Ousted as East German Leader." *Facts on File: World News Digest with Index* (Volume 49, No. 2552, October 20, 1989): 785.

15. Harold Klemp, *The Temple of ECK,* (Minneapolis: ECKANKAR, 1991).

16. Marcia Montenegro, "A Story of Walls." *Welcome to Planet Earth* (Volume 9, No. 6): 11.

17. *Information Please Almanac Atlas & Yearbook* (Boston: Houghton Mifflin Company, 1993)

Chapter 6. Reverberations from the Past

1. David Reed, "Sunken Treasure!" *Reader's Digest* (Large-type edition, December 1990): 62–74.

2. Ibid.

3. Paul Twitchell, *The ECK-Vidya, Ancient Science of Prophecy* (Minneapolis: ECKANKAR, 1972).

4. Philip Elmer-De Witt, "The Golden Treasures of Nimrud." *Time* (October 30, 1989): 80–81.

5. *The Mystic World,* Fall 1989.

6. *The Mystic World,* Winter 1989.

7. Philip Elmer-De Witt, "The Golden Treasures of Nimrud." *Time* (October 30, 1989): 80.

8. Ibid.

Chapter 7. Field of Dreams

1. Paul Twitchell, *The ECK-Vidya, Ancient Science of Prophecy* (Minneapolis: ECKANKAR, 1972).

2. Ibid.

3. Ibid.

Chapter 8. For All Mankind

1. Paul Twitchell, *The ECK-Vidya, Ancient Science of Prophecy* (Minneapolis: ECKANKAR, 1972).

2. Paul Twitchell, *The Shariyat-Ki-Sugmad,* Book Two (Minneapolis: ECKANKAR, 1971, 1988).

3. Samuel A. Schreiner, Jr., *Cycles* (New York: Donald I. Fine, Inc., 1990).

4. Ibid.

5. Ibid.

6. Paul Twitchell, *The ECK-Vidya, Ancient Science of Prophecy* (Minneapolis: ECKANKAR, 1972).

7. Ibid.

8. Ibid.

9. Samuel A. Schreiner, Jr., *Cycles* (New York: Donald I. Fine, Inc., 1990).

10. Ibid.

11. Paul Twitchell, *Difficulties of Becoming the Living ECK Master* (Menlo Park: Illuminated Way Publishing, 1980).

12. Neil F. Michelsen, *Tables of Planetary Phenomena* (San Diego: ACS Publications, Inc., 1990).

13. Ibid.

14. Ibid.

15. Paul Twitchell, *The Wisdom Notes,* (Menlo Park: ECKANKAR, 1980).

16. Neil F. Michelsen, *Tables of Planetary Phenomena* (San Diego: ACS Publications, Inc., 1990).

Chapter 9. Vision Quest Two: The Holy Fire

1. Paul Twitchell, *The Wisdom Notes* (Menlo Park: ECKANKAR, 1980).

2. Paul Twitchell, *The Shariyat-Ki-Sugmad,* Book One (Minneapolis: ECKANKAR, 1970, 1987).

3. Harold Klemp, "Awaken to ECK" audiocassette (Minneapolis: ECKANKAR, 1991).

4. *Administrative News, 101st Congress, Second Session* (Volume 2, 1990).

Chapter 10. Global Initiation

1. *The Mystic World,* Fall 1990.

2. Kent Durden, *Gifts of an Eagle,* (New York: Simon and Schuster, 1972).

Chapter 11. The Celestial Temple of ECK

1. Harold Klemp, *The Temple of ECK,* (Minneapolis: ECKANKAR, 1991).

2. Harold Klemp, *Child in the Wilderness* (Minneapolis: ECKANKAR, 1989).

3. Zecharia Sitchin, *The 12th Planet* (New York: Avon Books, 1978).

4. Ibid.

5. Paul Twitchell, *The ECK-Vidya, Ancient Science of Prophecy* (Minneapolis: ECKANKAR, 1972).

Chapter 12. The Universal Body of the Mahanta

1. Bertrand Russell, *History of Western Philosophy* (New York: Simon & Schuster Trade, 1984).

2. Ibid.

3. Ibid.

4. Ibid.

5. H. E. Huntley, *The Divine Proportion* (New York: Dover Publications, Inc., 1970).

6. Ibid.

7. Paul Twitchell, *The ECK-Vidya, Ancient Science of Prophecy* (Minneapolis: ECKANKAR, 1972).

8. Brinton, Christopher, and Wolff, *A History of Civilization: Volume One: to 1715,* Second Edition (Englewood Cliffs: Prentice-Hall, Inc., 1955, 1960).

9. Ibid.

10. Paul Twitchell, *The Spiritual Notebook* (Minneapolis: ECKANKAR, 1971, 1990).

11. György Doczi, *The Power of Limits* (Boston & London: Shambhala, 1985).

12. H. E. Huntley, *The Divine Proportion* (New York: Dover Publications, Inc., 1970).

13. Paul Twitchell, *The Far Country* (Minneapolis: ECKANKAR, 1971).

14. György Doczi, *The Power of Limits* (Boston & London: Shambhala, 1985).

15. Ibid.

16. Ibid.

17. David Calvo, "The Acorn Planter and the Temple of ECK." *The Mystic World* (September 1992): 3.

18. György Doczi, *The Power of Limits* (Boston & London: Shambhala, 1985).

19. Paul Twitchell, *The Shariyat-Ki-Sugmad,* Book Two (Minneapolis: ECKANKAR, 1971, 1988).

20. Ibid.

21. Ibid.

22. Ibid.

23. Ibid.

24. Paul Twitchell, *The ECK-Vidya, Ancient Science of Prophecy* (Minneapolis: ECKANKAR, 1972).

166

25. *The Mystic World,* Fall 1989.

26. H. E. Huntley, *The Divine Proportion* (New York: Dover Publications, Inc., 1970).

27. Paul Twitchell, *The Shariyat-Ki-Sugmad,* Book Two (Minneapolis: ECKANKAR, 1971, 1988).

How to Learn More about ECKANKAR
Religion of the Light and Sound of God

Why are you as important to God as any famous head of state, priest, minister, or saint that ever lived?

- Do you know God's purpose in your life?
- Why does God's Will seem so unpredictable?
- Why do you talk to God, but practice no one religion?

ECKANKAR can show you why special attention from God is neither random nor reserved for the few known saints. But it is for every individual. It is for anyone who opens himself to Divine Spirit, the Light and Sound of God.

People want to know the secrets of life and death. In response to this need Sri Harold Klemp, today's spiritual leader of ECKANKAR, and Paul Twitchell, its modern-day founder, have written a series of monthly discourses that give the Spiritual Exercises of ECK. They can lead Soul in a direct way to God.

Those who wish to study ECKANKAR can receive these special monthly discourses which give clear, simple instructions for the spiritual exercises.

Membership in ECKANKAR Includes

1. Twelve monthly discourses which include information on Soul, the spiritual meaning of dreams, Soul Travel techniques, and ways to establish a personal relationship with Divine Spirit. You may study them alone at home or in a class with others.
2. The *Mystic World,* a quarterly newsletter with a Wisdom Note and articles by the Living ECK Master. In it are also letters and articles from members of ECKANKAR around the world.
3. Special mailings to keep you informed of upcoming ECKANKAR seminars and activities worldwide, new study materials available from ECKANKAR, and more.
4. The opportunity to attend ECK Satsang classes and book discussions with others in your community.
5. Initiation eligibility.
6. Attendance at certain meetings for members of ECKANKAR at ECK seminars.

How to Find Out More

To request membership in ECKANKAR using your credit card (or for a free booklet on membership) call (612) 544-0066, weekdays, between 8:00 a.m. and 5:00 p.m., central time. Or write to: ECKANKAR, Att: Information, P.O. Box 27300, Minneapolis, MN 55427 U.S.A.

Introductory Books on ECKANKAR

The Dream Master
Mahanta Transcripts, Book 8
Harold Klemp

If you don't believe dreams are important, you're missing out on more than half your life. Harold Klemp, the Dream Master, can show you how to become more aware of your dreams so you can enjoy a better life. But *The Dream Master* is not just about dreams. It gives you the keys to spiritual survival, and is about living life to the fullest on your way home to God.

Earth to God, Come In Please . . .

Stories from ordinary people who have become aware of a greater force operating in their lives. Their experiences outside the commonplace brought lessons in love and spiritual freedom that changed them deeply. They show how we can make contact with the Voice of God, for spiritual knowledge and awareness beyond words.

The Secret Language of Waking Dreams
Mike Avery

Are you overlooking the countless ways life speaks to you for your benefit? This book guides you to a better understanding of your own secret inner language—the language of waking dreams. It will wake you up to what life is really trying to teach you!

HU: A Love Song to God
Audiocassette

Learn how to sing an ancient name for God, HU (pronounced like the word *hue*). A wonderful introduction to ECKANKAR, this two-tape set is designed to help listeners of any religious or philosophical background benefit from the gifts of the Holy Spirit. It includes an explanation of the HU, stories about how Divine Spirit works in daily life, and exercises to uplift you spiritually.

For fastest service, phone (612) 544-0066 weekdays between 8:00 a.m. and 5:00 p.m., central time, to request books using your credit card, or look under **ECKANKAR** in your phone book for an ECKANKAR Center near you. Or write: **ECKANKAR, Att: Information, P.O. Box 27300, Minneapolis, MN 55427 U.S.A.**

There May Be an
ECKANKAR Study Group near You

ECKANKAR offers a variety of local and international activities for the spiritual seeker. With hundreds of study groups worldwide, ECKANKAR is near you! Many areas have ECKANKAR Centers where you can browse through the books in a quiet, unpressured environment, talk with others who share an interest in this ancient teaching, and attend beginning discussion classes on how to gain the attributes of Soul: wisdom, power, love, and freedom.

Around the world, ECKANKAR study groups offer special one-day or weekend seminars on the basic teachings of ECKANKAR. Check your phone book under **ECKANKAR**, or call **(612) 544-0066** for membership information and the location of the ECKANKAR Center or study group nearest you. Or write **ECKANKAR, Att: Information, P.O. Box 27300, Minneapolis, MN 55427 U.S.A.**

☐ Please send me information on the nearest ECKANKAR discussion or study group in my area.

☐ Please send me more information about membership in ECKANKAR, which includes a twelve-month spiritual study.

Please type or print clearly   940

Name _____

Street _____ Apt. # _____

City _____ State/Prov. _____

Zip/Postal Code_____ Country _____